Instructor's Manual

to accompany

Building Classroom Discipline

Fifth Edition

C. M. Charles
San Diego State University

Prepared by

Gail W. Senter
California State University San Marcos

Longman Publishers USA

Instructor's Manual to accompany
Building Classroom Discipline, Fifth Edition

Longman, 10 Bank Street, White Plains, N.Y. 10606

Associated Companies:
Longman Group Ltd., London
Longman Cheshire Pty., Melbourne
Longman Paul Pty., Auckland
Copp Clark Longman Ltd., Toronto

ISBN: 0-8013-1507-7 Title Code: 76838 (Student Book)
ISBN: 0-8013-1644-8 Title Code: 77090 (Instructor's Manual)
ISBN: 0-8013-1708-8 Title Code: 77200 (Exam Pack)
ISBN: 0-8013-1707-X Title Code: 77201 (Transparency Pack)

1 2 3 4 5 6 7 8 9 10-VG-9998979695

INSTRUCTORS' MANUAL

to Accompany

BUILDING CLASSROOM DISCIPLINE, FIFTH EDITION

CONTENTS   Page

- **Main Focus of Building Classroom Discipline, Fifth Edition**
- Revisions, Organization, and New Features of the Fifth Edition
- Purpose and Organization of this Manual
- Identifying Major Outcomes for Your Course
- Planning Your Course Syllabus
- Alternative Organizational Plans
- Introducing the Textbook to Your Students
- Chapter-by-Chapter Presentation
- Using the Textbook's Appendixes and Bibliography

INTRODUCTION

MAIN FOCUS OF Building Classroom Discipline, Fifth Edition

This fifth edition of Building Classroom Discipline retains the purpose and focus of previous editions, which are to help individuals training to become elementary, middle school, and secondary teachers acquire skills for effective classroom discipline. The book will also be helpful to experienced teachers wishing to sharpen their skills in classroom control.

The book provides information to help teachers organize and implement effective discipline that is consonant with student needs, social realities, and the personal needs, beliefs, and styles of individual teachers.

To assist readers in the development of optimal discipline systems, ten widely acclaimed models of discipline are presented, along with illustrative scenarios, practice activities, and guided application opportunities. While these models are excellent in maintaining discipline, this book reflects the belief that the most effective discipline systems are those that teachers themselves compose.

REVISIONS, ORGANIZATION, AND NEW FEATURES OF THE FIFTH EDITION

New Models of Discipline

Previous editions presented eight models of discipline, selected for historical, theoretical, and/or practical value. This edition is expanded to ten models, reflecting newer developments receiving wide attention in classroom discipline. The two new models are those of (1) Thomas Gordon, developer of Parent Effectiveness Training (P.E.T.) and Teacher Effectiveness Training (T.E.T), whose views on discipline are presented in his 1989 book Discipline that Works: Promoting Self-Discipline in Children and (2) Richard Curwin and Allen Mendler, whose views on maintaining student dignity and restoring hope are expressed in their 1988 book Discipline with Dignity.

Reorganization of Models

This edition reorganizes the presentation of models into Part I and Part II. Part I is called "Foundation Models of Discipline" and includes four models rarely used today as complete discipline systems. These four models are important for having broken new ground and introduced new concepts and practical applications. In addition, they help chronicle the progression of developments in classroom discipline. The four foundation models are:

    The Redl and Wattenberg Model, the first to propose an organized approach to managing student behavior. Much of this work concentrated on how to deal with groups.

    The Neo-Skinnerian Model, which applied B. F. Skinner's principles of reinforcement in the development of behavior modification, used to shape desired behavior in the classroom.

    The Kounin Model, the first to stress the management of lessons, routines, and accountability as keys to classroom discipline.

The Ginott Model, the first to stress the importance of communication and addressing situations rather than students' character.

Part II, called "Application Models of Discipline," presents six models that are widely used today. Each of these models, while containing elements from the foundation models, contributes new concepts and practices and is able to serve as a complete system of discipline in itself. The six application models are:

The Dreikurs Model, which focuses on democratic teaching and dealing with students' mistaken goals which lead to misbehavior.

The Canter Model, which emphasizes teaching students how to behave responsibly and assertively following through to help them do so.

The Jones Model, which uses body language, meaningful incentives, and efficient help to enable students to control their own behavior.

The Glasser Model, which focuses on "lead teaching" (instead of "boss teaching"), on providing quality school experiences, and on helping students do quality work.

The Gordon Model, which helps teachers develop responsibility in students, understand "problem ownership," and apply the intervention strategies called for by problem ownership.

The Curwin and Mendler Model, which centers on providing needed help to students who are behaviorally at risk of failure by maintaining student dignity and restoring hope.

Guidance for Preparing Personal Systems of Discipline

As in previous editions, strong detailed guidance is presented for helping users develop their own personal systems of discipline. This specific guidance is provided in three chapters entitled:

"Classrooms That Encourage Good Behavior," which addresses the nature and importance of classroom climate, communication, routines, interactions, and other management concerns that affect responsible behavior.

"Building a Personal System of Discipline," which takes readers through eight detailed steps that lead to quality systems of discipline tailored to needs of students and teachers.

"Exemplars: Personal Systems of Discipline," which presents systems of discipline developed and used by outstanding teachers at the primary, intermediate, middle school, and high school levels. Also included are three specialty systems and one school-wide system. The number of exemplars has been increased from 8 in previous editions to 13 in this edition.

Illustrative Scenarios and Application Exercises

Each of the ten models of discipline contains vignettes or scenarios that help illustrate major concepts, expanded somewhat over previous editions. Application Exercises at the ends of chapters provide practice in applying selected concepts and techniques. Included for each chapter is a repetitive set of Concept Cases that allows readers to apply different models to the same instances of misbehavior, thereby facilitating comparison of the models.

Templates for Overhead Transparencies

Included in this manual are a number of templates for preparing overhead transparencies to facilitate discussions of chapter contents. The appropriate templates are presented with each chapter. They have been reduced to the size of this manual and should be enlarged on an enlarging copier before they are used to render transparencies.

Instructors' Discussion Notes

Sets of discussion notes are provided in this manual for assisting class discussions of the models and certain other chapters. These notes can be used without overhead transparencies but are coordinated with the transparency templates so that the two may be used in conjunction.

Comprehensive Lists of Concepts in Classroom Discipline

Appendix II contains a comprehensive list of discipline terms and concepts set forth in the ten models. They are alphabetized but presented without accompanying definitions, and can be used for self-appraisal and review.

Cumulative List of References and Recommended Readings

For easy reference, a cumulative list of all reference citations and recommended readings is presented in the Bibliography. References and readings pertinent to individual chapters are also presented at the end of each chapter.

PURPOSE AND ORGANIZATION OF THIS MANUAL

Purpose

This manual in intended to help accomplish the following:
- Describe the focus, nature, contents, and revisions in <u>Building Classroom Discipline, Fifth Edition</u>.
- Facilitate the organization and presentation of classes and workshops that use this book, by providing suggestions for course outcomes, syllabi, activities, assignments, and procedures for evaluation. Overhead transparency templates are provided, as are instructors' discussion notes for each content chapter. Alternate organizational plans are suggested for courses held in other than traditional schedules and time patterns.
- Provide a bank of true-false, multiple choice, and essay exam items. Answers to test items are given in each chapter of this manual.

In addition to information reviewed to this point, the manual presents the following:

Textbook Chapter Reviews

To provide refresher information and help with instructional planning, a summary of each chapter in Parts I and II is presented that explains major points and concepts, lists specific terms and their definitions, and when pertinent reviews strengths and shortcomings of the model.

Suggested Instructional Activities and Discussion Topics

Suggestions for activities are not intended to be prescriptive, but merely ideas for guiding students to deeper understandings of behavior management. Most instructors believe participants profit from multiple opportunities to reflect upon, analyze, discuss, and practice concepts and techniques. It is believed further that such activities assist participants later in planning their own personal systems of discipline.

Test Items

Test items for each chapter include true-false, multiple choice, and essay questions. True-false items depend mainly on recall and interpretation of information, while the multiple choice and essay call for deeper analysis and application. These test items are useful not only for weekly, midterm, and final examinations but for a variety of daily class activities and assignments, such as agree-disagree, exploring application of concepts, class debates, and initiators of discussions. The tests are presented on single pages in this manual so they can be duplicated easily on copy machines. Permission is expressly granted for duplicating the test materials in this manual.

Transparency Templates and Discussion Notes

Described earlier as a new feature, each chapter contains one or more templates for making overhead transparencies, plus a set of notes, correlated with the transparency template, for leading discussions concerning chapter contents.

IDENTIFYING MAJOR OUTCOMES FOR YOUR COURSE

Students like having expected course outcomes stated clearly. Whether classroom discipline is the sole focus of your course or one topic among several, your students will appreciate your stating unambiguously what you expect them to learn. Usually, the list of outcomes can be kept short and inclusive, rather than detailed and lengthy. Examples: (Students are expected to become able to--)
- Identify and explain (X number of) basic concepts in each model of discipline.
- Analyze and evaluate the models of discipline in light of student needs, teacher needs, and preferred teaching style.
- Organize a personal system of discipline that meets one's preferred style of teaching as well as the needs of students.

PLANNING YOUR COURSE SYLLABUS

Activities

Time considerations, scheduling, number of students, and personal preferences for guest presenters, video viewing, videotaping, and the like all affect how you will plan your course and syllabus. Because of such factors, no single way of organizing the course is advocated. The following are presented as suggestions you might find helpful:

- Select class content and activities that are practical and directly related to the outcomes you have stated. Students do not object to course work they find interesting and worthwhile, but they usually complain about work for which they can see little purpose. Many activities designed to assist understanding and application are included in the textbook's end-of-chapter exercises.
- Along with class lectures and discussions, consider using films, guest presenters, teacher panels, student presentations, group debates, and small-group collaborative work. Ask students to describe discipline tactics they are currently observing or have observed, describe the relationship of their observations to theories studied in class, and list unanswered questions they might have.
- Encourage students' reading from original sources, especially books by authors whose models of discipline are included in the text. Consider giving extra credit to those who read such works and make oral or written reports.
- Plan to have students meet with you individually during the term to discuss progress in developing their personal systems of discipline.

Evaluation Procedures

Evaluation activities that are normally effective include examinations and an end-of-course paper in which participants describe a personal discipline system they believe would serve them best. The examinations should be discussed with students and their number and nature mutually agreed upon. The major paper can be done adequately in about five typewritten pages, double spaced. Other evaluation procedures that might be considered include students' keeping notebooks in which they enter favorite ideas from the models of discipline and from other sources, students' making videotapes in which discipline techniques are shown, students keeping folders of class assignments, and students' doing outside reading and reporting for extra credit.

The specific procedures by which grades are assigned tend to be highly personal. Many instructors use criteria such as the following, which are presented as illustrations:

Class attendance and participation	25%
Chapter quizzes	25%
Paper on personal system of discipline	50%

or

Class attendance and participation	10%
Class folder	10%
Chapter quizzes	20%
Mid-term and final exams	30%
Paper on personal system of discipline	30%
Optional bonus for book report	1/3 letter grade
or Optional bonus for special project	1/3 letter grade

ALTERNATIVE ORGANIZATIONAL PLANS

Courses dealing with classroom discipline are typically delivered in four different organizational schemes: (1) normal semester devoted to discipline alone, (2) normal quarter devoted to discipline alone, (3) shorter workshop formats devoted solely to discipline, and (4) normal semester or quarter, in which discipline is one topic among others. The textbook has been designed to fit a semester calendar but is adaptable to other calendars as well.

For Semester Courses: Calendar Sequence:

Week 1: Introduction to course. Presentation of syllabus. Discussion of course requirements. Introduction of textbook. Lecture-discussion on discipline, concerns about discipline, and three facets of discipline. Briefly review each of the 10 models of discipline. Assign students to make later presentations on various models.

Week 2: The Redl and Wattenberg Model of Discipline. Use overheads and discussion notes. Class quiz. Complete activities at end of chapter and apply to related scenarios.

Week 3: The Neo-Skinnerian Model of Discipline. Quiz and appropriate activities.

Week 4: The Kounin Model of Discipline. Activities as appropriate.

Week 5: The Ginott Model of Discipline. Activities as appropriate.

Week 6: Exam over foundation models of discipline. The Dreikurs Model of Discipline. Activities as appropriate.

Week 7: The Canter Model of Discipline. Activities as appropriate.

Week 8: The Jones Model of Discipline. Activities as appropriate.

Week 9: The Glasser Model of Discipline. Activities as appropriate.

Week 10: The Gordon Model of Discipline. Activities as appropriate.

Week 11: The Curwin and Mendler Model of Discipline. Activities as appropriate.

Week 12: Exam over application models of discipline. Introduction to preparing a personal system of discipline, with activities as appropriate.

Week 13: Topic: Classrooms That Encourage Good Behavior. Activities as appropriate.

Week 14: In-class work on personal systems of discipline. Instructor assists as needed.

Week 15: Class reports for extra credit. Submission of final papers. Closure.

For Quarter Courses: Calendar Sequence

Week 1: Introduction to course. Presentation of syllabus. Discussion of course requirements. Introduction of textbook. Lecture-discussion on concerns about discipline, what discipline is, and three facets of discipline. Briefly review each of the 10 models of discipline. Assign students to make class presentations on models.

Week 2: The Redl and Wattenberg and Neo-Skinnerian Models. Activities as appropriate.

Week 3: The Kounin and Ginott Models. Activities as appropriate.

Week 4: Exam over foundation models. The Dreikurs Model. Activities as appropriate.

Week 5: The Canter and Jones Models. Activities as appropriate.

Week 6: The Glasser and Gordon Models. Activities as appropriate.

Week 7: The Curwin and Mendler Model. Activities as appropriate. Introduction to composing a personal system of discipline.

Week 8: Exam on application models of discipline. Topic: Classrooms that Encourage Good Behavior. Activities as appropriate.

Week 9: In-class work on preparing personal systems of discipline. Instructor monitors and assists.

Week 10: Class reports for extra credit. Submission of final papers. Closure.

For Shorter Workshops: Calendar Sequence for Five Sessions

Prior to the first meeting, contact students if possible and request that they look over the textbook and consider which of selected models they would like to study in depth.

First Evening Session:	Introduction and review of expectations. Exploration of the textbook.. Lecture on discipline, major concerns, and three facets of discipline.
Morning Session:	Presentations and application activities on selected foundation models. Guest presenter. Group cooperative work.
Afternoon Session:	Presentations and application activities on selected application models. Film or videotape. Student panels.
Morning Session:	Presentation and application activities related to difficult-to-manage students. Guest presenters experienced in working with the difficult-

to-manage. Group collaborative work on applying knowledge to selected scenarios in Appendix I. Review steps in building a personal system of discipline.

Afternoon Session: Class time used for work on personal system of discipline. Instructor works with participants and assists as needed.

Two Weeks Later: Personal systems of discipline are submitted. Instructor reviews the work, provides written feedback, and mails plans back to participants.

For Courses in which Discipline Is One of the Topics

If discipline is one topic considered in a broader course, it can be woven in by asking students to make themselves expert in selected models. Students then make presentations, instruct other students, and lead discussions concerning their model. Examinations and papers may be assigned as appropriate to the course.

INTRODUCING THE TEXTBOOK TO YOUR STUDENTS

Concern about Discipline

Mention that the first edition of this text was published in 1981 and that every year since that time teachers and the public have listed discipline among the top three concerns in public education. Use Transparencies 1 and 2 to launch the discussion.

Ultimate Purpose of the Text

Explain that the ultimate purpose of the textbook is to enable users to compose personal systems of discipline that they consider best for their students and themselves. The information needed for that purpose is presented in the various chapters.

Ten Acclaimed Models of Discipline

Point out that 10 acclaimed models of discipline are described and analyzed. The first four, the foundation models, are rarely used in their entirety today, but they have contributed significantly to the theory and practice of discipline. Use Transparency 3 to introduce the foundation models. The next six, the application models, are widely used today in classrooms at various levels. Use Transparency 4 to introduce these models. Additional chapters in the text focus on helping users develop personal systems of discipline.

Organization of Chapters

Show how the chapters are organized, especially the chapters on models of discipline--biographical sketch of model originator, primary focus of the model, key concepts and teachings, analysis of the model, strengths and shortcomings, and how the model is initiated or put into practice. Show that in order to facilitate learning of practical knowledge, each chapter also presents a set of concept cases and a number of Application exercises.

The Appendixes and Bibliography

Draw attention to Appendix I, which contains practice scenarios; Appendix II, a comprehensive alphabetized list of concepts and terms in discipline; and the Bibliography of references and recommended readings.

CHAPTER-BY-CHAPTER PRESENTATION

Abstracts, Terminology, and Appraisals of Models

For each chapter there is provided an abstract of major points, a list of concepts and teachings and their definitions, and when appropriate, an appraisal of the model's strengths and shortcomings.

Overhead Transparencies and Discussion Notes

For each chapter there is provided one or more templates for overhead transparencies and a set of discussion notes correlated with the transparencies. These are used to review and discuss chapter contents.

Suggested Activities

For each chapter there is provided a list of suggested instructional activities, usually having to do with assignment, quiz, discussion topics, group work, and guest presenter or use of media.

Test Items

For each appropriate chapter, three tests are provided--true-false, multiple choice, and essay. Each test is presented on a single page so that it can be duplicated conveniently on copy machines. Answers to the test items are provided in the section preceding the test pages.

USING THE TEXTBOOK'S APPENDIXES AND BIBLIOGRAPHY

The textbook includes two appendixes and a bibliography. Appendix I presents scenarios that depict classroom misbehavior for different subjects at different grade levels. These scenarios are very useful for practice in applying various discipline tactics. In using them one should ask:
1. What is the problem behavior? Who is bothered by it?
2. What seems to be causing the problem?
3. What should the teacher do to suppress the misbehavior?
4. What should the teacher do to redirect the misbehaving student?
5. What tactics should be used to maintain student self-respect and good human relations?

Appendix II presents a comprehensive list of concepts in classroom discipline. This list, provided without definitions, is very useful for end-of-course study and review.

The Bibliography presents a cumulative list of reference citations and recommended readings presented in each chapter. This bibliography can be used for instructional purposes, but is intended more for the benefit of instructors than of students.

BEHAVIOR AND MISBEHAVIOR

BEHAVIOR=ANYTHING A STUDENT CAN

DO

MISBEHAVIOR = BEHAVIOR THAT IS

INAPPROPRIATE

IN A PARTICULAR SITUATION.

TYPES OF CLASSROOM MISBEHAVIOR
(IN ORDER MOST LIKELY TO OCCUR)

GOOFING OFF

DISRUPTING CLASS

SPEAKING HURTFULLY TO OTHERS

NOT DOING ASSIGNED WORK

CHEATING OR LYING

REFUSING TO OBEY THE TEACHER

ATTACKING OTHERS PHYSICALLY

CLASSROOM DISCIPLINE

CLASSROOM DISCIPLINE = WHAT
TEACHERS DO
TO HELP STUDENTS BEHAVE
ACCEPTABLY
IN SCHOOL.

THREE FACETS OF CLASSROOM DISCIPLINE

PREVENTIVE DISCIPLINE

SUPPORTIVE DISCIPLINE

CORRECTIVE DISCIPLINE

WHAT IS MEANT BY MODELS OF DISCIPLINE

DEFINITION OF MODEL

FOUNDATION MODEL

APPLICATION MODEL

FOUNDATION MODELS
OF CLASSROOM DISCIPLINE

REDL & WATTENBERG 1951	DEALING WITH GROUPS TRAITS OF GROUPS GROUP DYNAMICS INFLUENCE TECHNIQUES
NEO-SKINNERIAN 1960	BEHAVIOR SHAPING OPERANT BEHAVIOR REINFORCEMENT BEHAVIOR MODIFICATION
KOUNIN 1971	MANAGING CLASSROOMS WITHITNESS ALERTING STUDENTS DELAYING SATIATION
GINOTT 1971	AUTHENTIC COMMUNICATION SANE MESSAGES INVITING COOPERATION CORRECTING BY DIRECTING

APPLICATION MODELS
OF CLASSROOM DISCIPLINE

DREIKURS 1972	GENUINE GOAL MISTAKEN GOALS DEMOCRATIC TEACHING INFLUENCE TECHNIQUES
CANTER 1976, 1992	TAKING CHARGE RIGHTS IN THE CLASSROOM TEACHING GOOD BEHAVIOR FOLLOWING THROUGH
JONES 1979, 1987	CONTROL VIA EFFICIENCY BODY LANGUAGE INCENTIVE SYSTEMS GIVING HELP EFFICIENTLY
GLASSER 1969, 1985, 1992	INVITATION VS. COERCION STUDENT NEEDS LEAD TEACHING QUALITY WORK
GORDON 1974, 1989	DEVELOPING SELF CONTROL BEHAVIOR WINDOW PROBLEM OWNERSHIP EFFECTIVE COMMUNICATION
CURWIN & MENDLER 1988, 1992	DISCIPLINE WITH DIGNITY BEHAVIORALLY AT RISK INVITING COOPERATION RESTORING HOPE

T4

Chapter 1

THE REDL AND WATTENBERG MODEL
Discipline through Dealing with the Group

CHAPTER ABSTRACT

Fritz Redl was born in Austria and educated there in psychology and psychiatry. After immigrating to the United States he entered into collaboration with William Wattenberg, an educational psychologist who shared Redl's interest in the relatively unexplored phenomena of group behavior.

The two men believed that humans continually attempt to protect and enhance the self, and in so doing behave differently when in groups than when alone or with one or two others. Those behavioral differences, they believed, come about through the interplay of psychological forces they called "group dynamics." In school classrooms, group dynamics produce behaviors that are often contrary to teacher expectations and therefore result in discipline problems.

Redl and Wattenberg claimed that teachers must understand the workings of group dynamics if they are to guide student behavior properly. Such understanding enables them to (1) identify roles students are likely to adopt (e.g. leader, clown, instigator, fall guy), (2) recognize conditions that produce contagious behavior, and (3) accept that most misbehavior results from students' trying to enhance or protect their sense of self.

Teachers can then deal effectively with misbehavior through using "diagnostic thinking" (hunch, facts, hidden factors, taking action, and remaining flexible), and employing appropriate "influence techniques" (supporting self-control, providing situational assistance, appraising reality, and invoking pleasure or pain).

These principles are set forth in Redl and Wattenberg's book Mental Hygiene in Teaching (New York: Harcourt, Brace & World, 1951, revised 1959), in which the authors maintain that both teachers and students can find greater enjoyment and success in school if they understand the factors that cause misbehavior and know how to deal with them humanely and effectively. As Redl and Wattenberg wrote:

> An understanding of [mental hygiene] should increase the likelihood that we can help all children develop into happier, more confident, and more stable adults. School life can become an ever more pleasant and significant part of young people's lives [and] teachers themselves can . . . obtain greater satisfaction from the hours spent earning a livelihood in the classroom. (1959, p. 23)

Although their model is now rarely used in its entirety, Redl and Wattenberg provided valuable information on group dynamics, and many of their ideas have been incorporated into more recent models of classroom discipline.

TERMINOLOGY

Group behavior--people in groups behave differently than they do individually. Group expectations influence individual behavior, and individual behavior in turn affects the group.

Student roles--within any group, various students adopt roles such as leaders, instigators, and fall guys. Teachers should be aware of the emergence of such roles and help limit the detrimental effects that some of them have.

Group dynamics--forces generated by and within groups strongly affect behavior. If teachers are to deal effectively with group behavior, they must understand these forces, how they develop, and how they affect behavior in the classroom.

Teacher roles--group behavior in the classroom is influenced by students' perceptions of the teacher. Students see teachers as filling many different roles. Teachers must be aware of those potential roles and what students expect of them.

Diagnostic thinking--in order to solve behavior problems correctly, teachers are encouraged to employ a diagnostic thinking process that involves (1) forming a first hunch, (2) gathering facts, (3) applying hidden factors (background information), (4) taking action, and (5) remaining flexible.

Influence techniques--teachers can correct student misbehavior and maintain class control by using influence techniques such as (1) supporting student self-control, (2) offering situational assistance, (3) appraising reality, and (4) invoking the pleasure-pain principle (reward and punishment).

Supporting student self-control--this control technique is low-keyed. Teachers address an emerging problem before it becomes serious, by using eye contact, moving closer to misbehaving students, providing encouragement, making use of humor, and in some cases simply ignoring minor misbehavior.

Providing situational assistance--this technique is also low-keyed. When students have difficulty regaining self control, teachers provide situational assistance by (1) helping students over a hurdle, (2) restructuring the time schedule, (3) establishing new routines, and (4) removing seductive objectives. Occasionally it might be necessary to (5) remove a student from the situation, or even (6) physically restrain a student.

Appraising reality--this control technique involves helping students understand the underlying causes of their misbehavior and foresee the consequences if they continue. Teachers speak openly and frankly about the situation and reemphasize existing limits on behavior, but at the same time they offer encouragement. In more severe cases, this is done in individual conferences with students.

Invoking the pleasure-pain principle--this control technique consists of rewarding good behavior and punishing bad behavior. Punishment should be used only as a last resort, however, because it is frequently counterproductive.

APPRAISAL OF THE MODEL

The major strength of the Redl and Wattenberg model is its explanation of how group psychology works, linked to a systematic approach for dealing positively with group behavior. The value of the model is further evident in the extent to which its principles and procedures have been incorporated into later models of discipline.

The major shortcoming of the model is its lack of a clear-cut procedure for dealing with more serious types of classroom behavior. Its procedures of diagnostic thinking and counseling are too time-consuming for efficient use in minute-to-minute teaching, even when teachers understand the procedures well.

INSTRUCTORS' DISCUSSION NOTES

Use Transparency 5 to guide discussion.

Redl and Wattenberg's Contributions to Classroom Discipline
    Developed the first widely recognized, systematic approach to classroom discipline
    Helped teachers understand dynamics of classroom behavior
    Showed importance of diagnosing behavior and situations
    Provided specific suggestions for dealing with misbehavior
    Pointed out negative aspects of harsh punishment

Group Behavior--Students behave differently in groups than individually. Groups assign roles to teachers and students and produce dynamics that affect the class's behavior positively and negatively. To be effective in discipline, teachers must assess those roles and dynamics and learn to deal appropriately with the behavior they engender.

Student Roles--roles that various students play in groups
    Leaders--natural and appointed; reflect group ideals; vary according to situation
    Clowns--class entertainers; help relieve tension; may disrupt learning unnecessarily
    Fall Guys--take undeserved blame to gain favor in the group; teachers should identify
        the real culprit
    Instigators--individuals who cause trouble but try to appear innocent; they should be
        identified and corrected

Group Dynamics--psychological forces that affect group behavior
    Contagious Behavior--students adopt misbehavior of another; should be squelched
    Scapegoating--group displaces hostility on unpopular member; should be stifled
    Teacher's Pets--group reacts with jealousy or anger if teacher appears to play
        favorites
    Reactions to Strangers--newcomers produce tension; group reactions are
        unpredictable
    Group Disintegration--group cohesion erodes over time; may increase misbehavior.

Psychological Roles of Teachers, as assigned by students
    Representatives of society; Judges; Source of knowledge; Helpers; Referees;
    Detectives; Models; Caretakers; Ego supporters; Group leaders; Surrogate parents;
    Targets for hostility; Friends and confidants; Objects of affection.
Group behavior is affected by which of these roles the group assigns to its teacher.

Control Techniques for Misbehavior--Redl and Wattenberg's two general types:
    1) Diagnostic Thinking--for quickly appraising the behavior situation
        a) Forming a first hunch--what is the probable cause?
        b) Gathering facts--what facts of behavior are evident?
        c) Exploring hidden factors--teacher reviews previous knowledge about
            students involved
        d) Taking action--teacher remediates the situation, in keeping with what is
        known
        e) Remaining flexible--teacher is ready to admit and correct mistakes or take
            new actions
    2) Applying Influence Techniques--what teacher does to resolve misbehavior
        a) Support student self-control, when behavior is not serious: Send signals; Use
            physical proximity; Show interest in student or work; Use humor
            appropriately (not hurtfully); Ignore minor infractions.
        b) Provide situational assistance, when student is unable to regain self-control
            Provide hurdle help; restructure or reschedule the activity; clarify routines;
            remove student from situation; remove seductive objects; physical restraint.
        c) Conduct reality appraisal--help students examine and reconsider their
    misbehavior; make frank appraisal; show encouragement; set clear enforceable
    limits
        d) Invoke the pleasure-pain principle--apply rewards and punishments
            appropriately
                Pleasure--praise and rewards, but Redl and Wattenberg downplay these
                Punishment--planned unpleasant consequences, but not harsh or
                abusive (Redl and Wattenberg go to some lengths to point out the
                undesirable side effects of harsh punishment.)

REDL & WATTENBERG'S VIEWS ON DISCIPLINE

Group Behavior

Student Roles

Group Dynamics

Psychological Roles of Teachers

Control Techniques for Misbehavior

SUGGESTED INSTRUCTIONAL ACTIVITIES

Assignment:

1. Read the chapter and do Application exercises as directed.

2. Begin the personal notebook into which entries are made for each model, to include:
- Ideas and suggestions you (the student) find appealing and compatible with your personality and philosophy.
- Ideas and suggestions with which you disagree.
- Your appraisal of the model as concerns its practicality and ease of implementation.

IT IS VERY IMPORTANT TO BEGIN THIS NOTEBOOK NOW AND MAKE ENTRIES FAITHFULLY. THIS WILL PROVIDE MOST OF WHAT YOU WILL ULTIMATELY NEED TO COMPLETE YOUR OWN PERSONAL SYSTEM OF DISCIPLINE.

Short Quiz (to ensure careful reading).

Discussion Topics

1. What do think about Redl and Wattenberg's depiction of group behavior? Does it correspond to what you have observed? Have you seen students enacting the roles described? Where? What were the results?

2. To what extent do you agree with Redl and Wattenberg that student behavior is strongly influenced by the way the teacher is perceived, that is, by the roles assigned to or played by the teacher? To what extent do you think the teacher can or should control this phenomenon? Can you illustrate with examples?

3. Redl and Wattenberg strongly advise teachers to use diagnostic thinking as they deal with misbehavior. What is your opinion, generally, about that process? How significant do you consider first hunch, fact gathering, and hidden factors to be?

4. Redl and Wattenberg urge teachers to "put themselves in the students' place" as concerns feelings. Other authorities do not necessarily agree. To what extent do you think student feelings should be considered when teachers have to control misbehavior?

5. Redl and Wattenberg advise using four categories of influence techniques. What is the purpose of the first technique, and what does it entail? The second? Third? Fourth?

6. What do Redl and Wattenberg have to say about, first, the nature of punishment (what it is/ should be) and second, the effect that harsh punishment is likely to have? Do you agree with them? Have you seen exceptions?

7. How do you judge the Redl and Wattenberg model in terms of probable effectiveness and ease of implementation?

8. Whether or not you agree with Redl and Wattenberg's suggestions as an overall approach to discipline, have you learned information that you think will be helpful in working with groups of students? Be specific.

Small-Group Collaborative Work

1. In groups of four or five, analyze Concept Cases 2, 3, and 4, at the end of the chapter. Indicate how Redl and Wattenberg would have you deal with the situations depicted. Present conclusions for class discussion.

2. Analyze Scenarios 2 and 8 in Appendix I. Indicate how the Redl and Wattenberg model would be applied to those situations. Present conclusions for class discussion.

TEST ITEMS

The following pages furnish true-false, multiple choice, and essay examination items related to the Redl and Wattenberg model. Permission is granted to duplicate them for classroom use. Answers:

True-False: 1.F, 2.T, 3.T, 4.F, 5.T, 6.F, 7.F, 8.T, 9.T, 10.T, 11.T, 12.F, 13.F, 14.F, 15.F, 16.T, 17.T, 18.T, 19.F, 20.F

Multiple Choice: 1.a, 2.d, 3.c, 4.b, 5.a, 6.c, 7.a, 8.b, 9.b, 10.a, 11.b, 12.c, 13.d, 14.c, 15.a, 16.a, 17.c, 18.c, 19.d, 20.d

Essay Answers

1. (a) Group dynamics accounts for role availability and function; students adopt roles to try to gain a sense of acceptance and belonging.
    (b) Leader (influences others to follow); clown (provides comic relief); instigator (initiates misbehavior but pretends not to be a part of it); fall guy (accepts blame and punishment, even when not deserved).

2. (a) to identify causes of misbehavior, best approaches for dealing with it, and likely outcomes of correction.
    (b) first hunch (educated guess), gather facts (what is observable), assess hidden factors (conditions, motivations, not readily apparent), acting (applying influence techniques), remaining flexible (ready to reassess situation, attempt another solution).

3. (a) main purpose is to guide student behavior positively, whether individual or group; equally important purpose is to make life pleasant and productive for students and teacher alike.

(b) support self-control (signals, proximity, show interest, ignore), provide situational assistance (hurdle help, restructuring, establish routines, remove seductive objects) reality appraisal (tell it like it is with clarity, encouragement, limit-setting).

(c) punishment can harm student self-concept, reduce student self-direction, harms relations with the teacher, and presents an undesirable model for solving problems.

4. (a) instructor judgment concerning five elements and conclusions in diagnostic thinking

(b) instructor judgment concerning aspects of supporting self-control, providing situational assistance, reality appraisal.

ESSAY EXAM: Write your responses to the following items as directed.

1. Regarding student "roles" in the class:

(a) Explain why many students adopt roles in the class.

(b) List four typical student roles and describe their characteristics.

2. Describe "diagnostic thinking" in the classroom, as concerns:

(a) its purpose

(b) the elements it includes and the characteristics of each element

3. Supporting self-control, providing situational assistance, appraising reality, and invoking the pleasure-pain principle are four categories of influence techniques. Describe each in terms of

(a) its main purpose,

(b) three specific techniques, briefly explained, for each of the first three categories,

(c) the cautions concerning punishment in the pleasure-pain category.

4. You have in your class Susan, a motivated and intelligent student who usually does her work as assigned. Today instead of working she is talking and laughing with another student.

(a) Describe your diagnostic thinking procedure and the conclusions to which it leads.

(b) Based on your diagnosis, describe in order the first three things you would do to try to get her back to work (assuming that each of your attempts was unsuccessful).

Name_____Date_____

The items on this page all relate to the REDL AND WATTENBERG model. Answer true or false, as directed.

1. Group behavior is best understood through analysis of individual behavior.

2. Group behavior is influenced by how students perceive the teacher.

3. "Taking action" in diagnostic thinking means using what are called "influence techniques."

4. Redl and Wattenberg say teachers should not use punishment, which is counterproductive.

5. "Appraising reality" helps students foresee probable consequences of their behavior.

6. When appraising reality, teachers move closer to the misbehaving student and simply say nothing.

7. Invoking the"pleasure-pain principle" involves ignoring students whose behavior is disruptive.

8. One characteristic of group leaders is that they usually embody group ideals.

9. "Instigators" try to give the appearance that they are not involved in misbehavior.

10. "Fall guys" willingly accept blame for what they did not do as a way of gaining favor in the group.

11. Students play roles in the group because it helps them feel accepted.

12. Group dynamics are exercises in communicating and relating that teachers use to build group spirit.

13. If a particular misbehavior appears to be very contagious, the teacher should ignore it at first.

14. Unfortunately, desirable classroom behavior is rarely contagious.

15. Teachers are usually the main target of student scapegoating.

16. Teachers should expect group relationships to disintegrate over time, though not irreparably.

17. Group dynamics may produce classroom behavior that differs from what teachers expect.

18. Teachers do not have full control over the psychological roles their students assign them.

19. "Source of knowledge" is a psychological role that students rarely assign their teacher.

20. Diagnostic thinking is described by Redl and Wattenberg as identifying "who did what to whom."

Name_____Date_____

All items relate to the REDL AND WATTENBERG model. Mark the single best answer for each item as directed.

1. Redl and Wattenberg liken the classroom group to a/an (a) organism, (b) individual, (c) clan, (d) partnership.
2. NOT listed as a common classroom role was (a) clown, (b) instigator, (c) fall guy, (d) enforcer.
3. Group dynamics means (a) ambivalence, (b) excitement, (c) psychological forces, (d) argumentation.
4. One onto whom hostility is displaced: (a) instigator, (b) scapegoat, (c) isolate, (d) fall guy.

5. Positive benefits are often produced by (a) clown, (b) instigator, (c) fall guy, (d) teacher's pet.
6. A step in diagnostic thinking: (a) analysis, (b) enforcement, (c) acting, (d) closure.

7. In diagnostic thinking, teachers should be (a) flexible, (b) sure, (c) adamant, (d) humorous.

8. In diagnostic thinking, teachers should remember (a) aspirations, (b) feelings, (c) whims, (d) roadblocks.
9. "Influence techniques" are involved in: (a) hunch, (b) acting, (c) analysis, (d) facts.

10. Before correcting misbehavior, teachers should consider (a) motivation, (b) closure, (c) effort, (d) penalty.
11. Signals and proximity support (a) reality, (b) self control, (c) assistance, (d) diagnosis.

12. Proximity control is considered (a) offensive, (b) coercive, (c) low-key, (d) ineffective.

13. Teacher sarcasm (a) is acceptable as humor, (b) builds camaraderie, (c) is always hurtful, (d) is very dangerous.
14. Foreseeing probable consequences is central to (a) fact gathering, (b) misbehavior cause, (c) reality appraisal, (d) group dynamics.
15. Instead of criticizing students, teachers should (a) encourage, (b) ignore misbehavior, (c) invoke pain or pleasure, (d) use threats as promises.
16. Teachers should use punishment (a) as a last resort, (b) in reality appraisal, (c) in diagnostic thinking, (d) in demonstrating class rules.
17. The "pain principle" should be depicted as a (a) threat, (b) motivator, (c) promise, (d) cure.
18. "Setting limits" means (a) invoking pleasure-pain, (b) explaining punishments, (c) describing acceptable behavior, (d) increasing motivation.
19. Punishment should be seen as (a) physical, (b) spiteful, (c) unforgivable, (d) a consequence.
20. Redl and Wattenberg focus on behavior of (a) triads, (b) singles, (c) partners, (d) groups.

Chapter 2

THE NEO-SKINNERIAN MODEL
Discipline through Shaping Desired Behavior

CHAPTER ABSTRACT

Learned behavior is shaped by what happens to an individual immediately after performing a particular act. Many principles of behavior shaping have been discovered, and practices derived from them have been developed. Those principles and practices can be understood and applied easily, giving teachers powerful techniques for influencing student behavior and learning.

Most of the principles of behavior shaping were formulated through research by B. F. Skinner, and though he himself never proposed that they be used in school discipline, many of his followers (the Neo-Skinnerians) have done so.

Behavior shaping (called "behavior modification" when used systematically in classrooms) rests on the fundamental belief that people try to do what brings them pleasure and try to avoid that which does not.

The key element in behavior modification is a process called "reinforcement," the application of reinforcing stimuli. In Skinner's terminology, a "reinforcer" is any stimulus that when applied immediately after an individual performs a given act increases the likelihood that the individual will repeat that act. (Reinforcers are often called "rewards," a term Skinner rejected as too vague for scientific use. Most people also assume that reinforcers bring pleasure to the recipient; again, Skinner assiduously avoided reference to emotions in his search into what he hoped would become a science of behavior.)

Good classroom behavior can be built through providing reinforcers when students behave desirably. When students misbehave, they receive no reinforcement, and over time the unacceptable behavior disappears (is extinguished). Punishment (not the same as negative reinforcement) also tends to weaken undesired responses and may in extreme cases be used to suppress misbehavior that is strongly ingrained. Behavior is shaped and maintained effectively as reinforcement is supplied in keeping with certain schedules. As a new learning is introduced, reinforcement is given after each small improvement by the student. Later, to maintain the learning, only intermittent reinforcement is required.

Years of experience have shown that most new learnings, academic or behavioral, can be shaped quickly through reinforcement. Ingrained behaviors may prove resistant to change. But even so, diligent use of behavior modification enables teachers, over time, to bring about the kind of classroom discipline that best serves everyone concerned.

TERMINOLOGY

Behavior shaping--the systematic use of reinforcing stimuli to change behavior in desired directions.

Operant behavior--any voluntary action that an individual performs.

Reinforcer--any stimulus received by an individual following a particular act (operant) that causes the individual to repeat the act.

Reinforcement--the process of supplying reinforcing stimuli.

Positive reinforcement--the process of furnishing a stimulus that causes an act to be repeated.

Negative reinforcement--the process of removing a stimulus, resulting in the act's being repeated. (Negative reinforcement is not the same as punishment.)

Schedules of reinforcement--the timing and frequency of supplying reinforcement.

Constant reinforcement--a schedule in which reinforcement is given every time an individual performs a desired act.

Intermittent reinforcement--a schedule in which reinforcement is given only occasionally.

Successive approximations--a behavior-shaping progression in which behavior comes closer and closer to the desired result.

Extinction--the disappearance of a behavior due to lack of reinforcement.

Behavior modification--a name commonly given to the overall process used to shape behavior.

Social reinforcers--words, gestures, and facial expressions that students desire.

Graphic reinforcers--marks and symbols of various kinds desired by students.

Activity reinforcers--activities that students enjoy sufficiently that they will do other work first or behave as desired in order to obtain them.

Tangible reinforcers--real objects that serve as reinforcers.

Contingency management--highly organized procedures of behavior modification in which students know they must do certain work or perform certain behaviors in order to earn reinforcement; these procedures typically make use of tangible reinforcers.

28

APPRAISAL OF THE NEO-SKINNERIAN MODEL

The main strength of the Neo-Skinnerian model is that behavior modification works, and works well. Without question it can promote better student behavior and more rapid learning. All teachers use it to some extent (they use praise and marks as reinforcers), but few do so systematically.

The shortcomings of behavior modification are that (1) it is too elaborate to be used comfortably throughout the day; (2) most teachers resist its full application as being either akin to bribing students to get them to learn and behave, or as overly manipulative, or as subversive to students' exercise of free will; and (3) unless punishment is included, behavior modification is ineffective for dealing with blatant misbehavior such as defiance and physical aggression.

Thus, behavior modification is most effective in the preventive and supportive aspects of discipline while relatively weak in corrective discipline.

INSTRUCTORS' DISCUSSION NOTES

Use Transparency 6 to guide discussion.

Neo-Skinnerians -- Those who followed and built upon B. F. Skinner's theories about how human behavior is formed.

The Neo-Skinnerians' Contributions to Classroom Discipline
   Showed how to use reinforcement to form desirable behavior in students.
   Showed the power of light, social reinforcement in shaping student behavior.
   Helped teachers be more positive and humane in controlling student behavior.

How Behavior is Shaped
   Operant Behavior--the student performs an act. If the act is appropriate, it is followed by a reinforcing stimulus.
      Reinforcing Stimulus (reinforcer)--something the teacher provides (positive reinforcement) or takes away (negative reinforcement) that makes the student more likely to repeat the act.
      Successive Approximations--gradual improvements that build toward the desired overall behavior
      Schedules of Reinforcement--constant, given every time the act is performed; this is good for promoting rapid learning, or intermittent, given occasionally but unpredictably after a particular act is performed; this is good for maintaining desired behavior.
      Extinction--no reinforcement is given, which causes the behavior gradually to disappear, to become extinguished.

Types of Reinforcers (Reinforcing Stimuli) Useful in Behavior Modification
Social--words (good, nice going, thank you) or behaviors (smiles, nods, thumbs-up)
Graphic--marks such as stars, checkmarks, smiley faces
Activity--activities that students especially enjoy, such as art, caring for the pet,
watching a videotape, or talking with a friend
Tangible--objects such as badges, decals, notes, pencils, certificates

Systems of Behavior Modification in the Classroom
Catch 'em Being Good--The teacher watches and, when students are seen behaving
desirably, provides appropriate reinforcement.
Rules-Ignore-Praise--Class rules of behavior are established. Students who break the
rules are ignored. Students who follow the rules are reinforced with praise.
Rules-Reward-Punishment--Class rules of behavior are established. Students who
follow the rules are reinforced. Students who break the rules are punished.
Token Economies--These are elaborate behavior modification plans that involve the
systematic use of graphic and tangible reinforcers (tokens) that can be
accumulated and cashed in for prizes.
Contracting--These are formalized, written behavior agreements that spell out target
behaviors, reinforcers, and time lines. They are signed by teacher and student and
made known to parents.

Planning for Behavior Modification
Analysis--Studying the picture of classroom behavior to identify what specifically is
going wrong (concerns), what might be causing the problem (antecedents), and
the kind of behavior, overall, that is desired.
Developing the Plan--Identification of target behaviors (the desired behaviors) and the
rules, reinforcers, and consequences that will be used to promote those behaviors.
Implementing the Plan--(a) The undesirable antecedent conditions are corrected, (b)
rules are reviewed and clarified, (c) consequences are described, (d) lessons are
tightened to reduce dead time, (e) instructional activities are made as interesting as
possible, and (f) the entire process is discussed with students and taught to them
as necessary.

NEO-SKINNERIANS - SELECTED EMPHASES IN CLASSROOM DISCIPLINE

How Behavior Is Shaped

Types of Reinforcers Useful in Behavior Modification

Systems of Behavior Modification in the Classroom

Planning for Behavior Modification

SUGGESTED INSTRUCTIONAL ACTIVITIES

Assignment

1. Read the chapter and complete the Application exercises as directed.

2. Make notebook entries on the Neo-Skinnerian model.

Quiz over the assigned reading.

Discussion Topics

1. You probably remember from psychology classes that Skinner often used pigeons in his research and that through reinforcement taught them to perform many complex acts, even to play table tennis. We can suppose that Skinner, who was educated in literature, might easily have said "All the world's a stage, and all the men and women merely pigeons." Had he said that, what might he have meant? (Ans: That practically all human behavior is learned; that we learn to play human roles; that human learning is described through the same principles as is pigeon learning.)

2. Many teachers when reintroduced to behavior modification say,"Oh, there is nothing new there; I always do that anyway." Yet their students may be behaving poorly or not learning as quickly as desired, and when their classes are observed it is discovered that the teachers are not using behavior modification as intended. What mistakes in its application are they most likely to be making?

3. Although Neo-Skinnerians have quite a different point of view on behavior management from that of Redl and Wattenberg, they do agree rather closely with Redl and Wattenberg concerning punishment. Explain how they agree and why.

4. Which do you think is more effective for adolescent learners, graphic reinforcers or activity reinforcers? Explain.

5. The class has become restive, with many students no longer paying attention. The teacher says, "Oh thank you, Clarisse, for sitting up so nicely and paying attention!" What effect would this probably have in a first-grade classroom? In a high school classroom?

6. Briefly differentiate between "Catch 'em Being Good," "Rules-Ignore-Praise," and "Rules-Reward-Punishment."

7. Have you ever seen a "token economy" used in the classroom? Explain how it was done.

8. Many teachers at all levels use "contracts," wherein individual students agree to behave in certain ways or complete specified work. Have you seen contracts used in this way? What do you think might be their strengths? Their shortcomings?

9. We have now examined two models of discipline, rather different from each other. Explain how they are alike or different with regard to:
   -What the teacher attempts to do in order to
      improve student behavior.
   -The extent to which student behavior is to be
      permanently changed (not just suppressed or redirected).
   -The models' ease of implementation in the classroom.

10. To what extent do you think the Redl and Wattenberg and the neo-Skinnerian models complement each other--that is, can they be melded together so as to make one model that is stronger than each might be individually? Explain.

Small-Group Activities

1. Determine how behavior modification would be used in dealing with Sara (Case 2) and Joshua (Case 3). Assign roles and role-play application of the techniques. Call on one or more of the groups to present their role-play to the class.

2. Analyze Scenarios 1, 4, 5, 6, and 7 in Appendix I. Specify how behavior modification might be used to improve behavior in each. Present the groups' conclusions to the class for discussion.

Guest Presentation

Invite two teachers who regularly use behavior modification to speak to the class. A regular classroom teacher and a special-education teacher make a good combination, as they normally use behavior modification differently and for different purposes.

TEST ITEMS

The following pages present items for true-false, multiple choice, and essay examinations. Permission is granted to duplicate the items for classroom use. Answers are given here.

True-False: 1.F, 2.F, 3.F, 4.F, 5.T, 6.F, 7.T, 8.F, 9.T, 10.F, 11.F, 12.T, 13.T, 14.F, 15.F, 16.T, 17.T, 18.T, 19.F, 20.T

Multiple Choice: 1.b, 2.c, 3.a, 4.a, 5.b, 6.d, 7.c, 8.a, 9.b, 10.c, 11.a, 12.d, 13.b, 14.d, 15.a, 16.c, 17.d, 18.b, 19.a, 20.c

Essay

1. The fundamental concept is the same (we do what brings us pleasure and avoid that which doesn't)but the two are installed with different purposes and procedures in mind. Behavior modification is used systematically, carefully, precisely, in attempting to shape desired behavior over time. Redl and Wattenberg's pleasure-pain is invoked only when misbehavior occurs. It is

33

intended as a correction, not a beginning-to-end learning assist. Also, pleasure-pain gives most of the attention to pain, as a suppresser, while behavior modification gives most of the attention to pleasure, as a motivator.

2. (a) Explain what is desired; lay out steps in the procedure; communicate reinforcers (and punishers if included); systematically reinforce both individually and collectively as behavior improves. (This procedure depends heavily on reinforcement.)

(b) Leave reward and punishment out altogether. Instead, discuss the problem; explain why improvement is needed; involve the students to reach agreement and obtain their support; make improvement a point of class pride; when breakdowns occur hold discussions to determine what has gone wrong and how improvements can be made.

3. (a) Criterion: instructor judgment concerning appropriateness of target behaviors specified.

(b) Either catch 'em being good, RIP, RRP, contingency management, and/or contracting.

(c) Criterion: instructor judgment concerning appropriateness of reinforcers for specified grade level or subject, and compatibility of reinforcers with the behavior modification plan chosen.

(d) Instructor judgment concerning description of successive approximations.

If procedure occurs faster than anticipated, give verbal reinforcement to class and change reinforcement schedule to intermittent.

If procedure occurs more slowly than anticipated, increase strength of reinforcers; or incorporate punishers; or change to more powerful punishers.

Name_____ Date_____
All items refer to the NEO-SKINNERIAN model. Mark each item true or false, as directed.

1. Skinner focused mainly on how the mind works and the roles it adopts to earn reinforcement.
2. Skinner was not interested in applying his findings to human beings; he left that to others.

3. Skinner's book <u>Beyond Freedom and Dignity</u> outlined the important role of free will in human behavior.
4. Behavior is usually shaped by the stimulus applied just before a response occurs.

5. Behavior can be weakened by both punishment and lack of reinforcement.

6. Unlike Redl and Wattenberg, Skinner was a strong advocate of using punishment to shape behavior.
7. Behavior modification typically relies on systematic reinforcement.

8. "Operant behavior" means approximately the same thing as reinforcement of behavior.

9. A slap is a positive reinforcer if it makes an individual more likely to repeat the behavior.

10. The term "successive approximations" refers to efforts to find the best levels of reinforcement.
11. Negative reinforcement reduces the likelihood that an individual will repeat the act being reinforced.
12. Punishment works more quickly than does positive reinforcement in stopping an undesired behavior.
13. Behavior modification is good for speeding the learning of academic material.

14. Giving the thumbs-up sign can fall into the category of "activity reinforcers."

15. Being allowed to work with a friend is a good example of tangible reinforcement.

16. In rules-ignore-praise behavior modification, it is the misbehavior that is ignored.

17. Older students generally judge the rules-reward-punishment type of behavior modification to be fair.
18. Contingency management and token economies have much in common.

19. Contracting is a most effective way of modifying behavior because the contracts are legally binding.
20. Target behaviors are defined as the new behaviors that one wishes to see exhibited by students.

Name_____ Date_____
All items relate to the NEO-SKINNERIAN model. Mark the single best answer, as directed.

1. Human behavior is shaped most by (a) punishment, (b) reinforcement, (c) operants,
    (d) free will.
2. To shape good behavior, teachers should use (a) rules, (b) smiles, (c) rewards, (d) threats.

3. Behavior is shaped by (a) consequences, (b) mind, (c) motivation, (d) immediate
    approximations.
4. Skinner's principles in use: (a) behavior modification, (b) operants, (c) stimuli,
    (d) approximation.
5. Specific behavior is weakened by (a) reinforcement, (b) punishment, (c) pleasure,
    (d) negativism.
6. Term for voluntary action: (a) approximation, (b) reinforcement, (c) reward, (d) operant.

7. Commonly used to mean reinforcement: (a) token, (b) contingency, (c) reward,
    (d) management.
8. Most students consider "Rules-Reward-Punishment" to be (a) fair, (b) unjust,
    (c) unreasonable, (d) hard.
9. Identifying behavior to be changed is done through (a) target, (b) analysis, (c) insight,
    (d) ignoring.
10. Punishment is used in (a) catch 'em being good, (b) RIP, (c) RRP, (d) negative
    reinforcement.
11. Specific work or behavior is written out in (a) contracts, (b) successive approximations,
    (c) antecedents, (d) catch 'em being good.
12. A term for desired behaviors: (a) antecedents, (b) implements, (c) consequences,
    (d) targets.
13. An example of an "activity reinforcer": (a) token, (b) talk, (c) sticker, (d) thumbs-up sign.

14. Used least frequently by teachers: (a) positive reinforcement, (b) verbal reinforcement,
    (c) graphic reinforcement, (d) negative reinforcement.
15. In contracts, teacher and student both usually (a) sign, (b) reinforce, (c) punish,
    (d) self-reward.
16. Behavior modification is criticized as being (a) too lenient, (b) too punitive, (c) too
    manipulative, (d) too dependent on free will.
17. The teacher's smile as a reinforcer: (a) graphic, (b) activity, (c) token, (d) nonverbal.

18. In classroom practice, reinforcement is (a) seldom used, (b) often used, (c) resisted by
    most teachers, (d) usually demanded by parents.
19. "Catch 'em being good" is most effective at which of these grade levels? (a) 1, (b) 6,
    (c) 9, (d) 12.
20. The reinforcement process: (a) stimulus-response, (b) Pavlovian, (c) operant-stimulus,
    (d) Freudian.

Essay Exam: Write out your answers to the following items, as directed.

1. It is sometimes said that behavior modification is nothing more than the application of the pleasure-pain principle that Redl and Wattenberg included in their model. Comment on that observation: Are the two the same? Are they similar but with differences? Are they completely different, both in concept and in application? Explain how you arrived at your conclusion.

2. The principles developed out of Skinner's research were built mainly from observations of pigeons and rats. Critics claim that humans, unlike laboratory animals, have reasoning power and that they therefore do not behave as do animals, especially when it comes to more complex behavior. Consider, as an example, a teacher's attempt to eradicate swearing in the classroom:
   (a) Make your best argument in support of behavior modification in assisting this process;
   (b) Make your best argument against the use of behavior modification in this process.

3. Suppose you decided to implement a behavior modification plan for the purpose of improving behavior in your classroom. Indicate the grade level, if elementary, or the subject area if secondary, and then:
   (a) Specify five target behaviors appropriate for your grade level or subject and tell how you will communicate them to your students;
   (b) Name the type of behavior modification plan you intend to use and explain why you have selected it;
   (c) List the specific reinforcers you intend to use, and:
   (d) Comment on how you foresee the process of successive approximations taking place (how the behavior will gradually change and how long it will take). Indicate changes you might make in your plan if the progress occurs faster than anticipated or more slowly than anticipated.

Chapter 3

THE KOUNIN MODEL
Discipline through Classroom Management

CHAPTER ABSTRACT

Jacob Kounin was the first educational psychologist to study carefully the effects of classroom management on student behavior. Unlike Redl and Wattenberg, he gave no attention to psychological forces operating within individuals or groups but attended only to cause-effect relationships between teacher acts and student behaviors.

Kounin videotaped hundreds of classrooms and from those tapes analyzed the behaviors of teachers and students. That enabled him to pinpoint teacher behaviors that increased class involvement in lessons while reducing misbehavior.

Kounin found that teachers' most effective management techniques were (1) using instructional variety coupled with intellectual challenge, (2) carefully pacing lessons and smoothing transitions between them, (3) demonstrating continual awareness of students' behavior, (4) attending to more than one issue at the same time, and (5) maintaining group focus. In Discipline and Group Management in Classrooms (New York: Holt, Rinehart & Winston, 1970) he wrote:

> There are different dimensions of group management that far outweigh disciplinary techniques in their power to influence the behavior of children in classrooms . . . and the correlations between teachers' styles . . . and children's behavior are higher than those obtained in previous studies between any attribute or behavior of teachers and any kind of consequence in children. (p. vii)

Kounin's contributions have proved to be among the most valuable ever made in school discipline, as evidenced by the numerous references to his work in educational literature and the extent to which his ideas have been incorporated into other models of discipline.

TERMINOLOGY

Ripple effect--a phenomenon in which teacher correction aimed at one particular student also affects the behavior of others in the class.

Withitness--teachers' demonstrating their awareness of what is going on in all parts of the classroom at all times (eyes in the back of the head).

Overlapping--the teacher's attending to two or more issues at the same time.

Movement management--the pacing and momentum within lessons and the transition from one lesson to another (has nothing to do specifically with physical movement of teacher or students).

Pacing--keeping an activity going at the most effective speed.

Momentum--keeping an activity moving forward.

Transition--moving from one activity to the next, or from one lesson to another.

Jerkiness--roughness in making transitions, leaving students confused as to what is expected of them.

Slowdowns--delays within and between activities that waste time and encourage misbehavior.

Group focus--keeping all students paying attention at the same time.

Group format--size and composition of the group (for purposes of lesson focus and active participation).

Student accountability--teachers' efforts to keep students on their toes and involved in lessons. Satiation--students' getting too much of an activity, which produces boredom and reluctance to participate.

APPRAISAL OF KOUNIN'S MODEL

The major strengths of the Kounin model are that it (1) clarifies the relationship between teacher management of lessons and student behavior and (2) details troublesome aspects of lesson management, thus paving the way for teacher improvement.

The major shortcoming of the Kounin model is that it provides virtually no help in dealing with misbehavior that is certain to occur, even in well-managed classes.

Thus, the Kounin model is very effective in the prevention of misbehavior but incomplete as an overall system of discipline because it does not provide guidance to help teachers correct misbehavior.

INSTRUCTORS' DISCUSSION NOTES

Use Transparency 7 to guide discussion.

Kounin's Contributions to Classroom Discipline
First to clarify the crucial roles that good classroom management and good lesson
management play in discipline
First to specify effects of "lesson movement" -- momentum and smoothness
Identified (and provided the label for) "withitness," a key factor in discipline
Reiterated the importance to discipline of maintaining student interest, gaining
attention, and holding students accountable for learning

The Ripple Effect--When teachers correct a student, the effect "ripples out" and causes
other students to behave better.
In primary grades--Ripple effect is pronounced; teachers make good use of it--
(Give examples.)
Among older students--Ripple effect is weak; not a useful technique in discipline.

Withitness--The teacher knows what is going on in all parts of the classroom at all times.
Students quickly recognize whether teachers possess this trait, and adjust their
behavior accordingly. Three important indicators of withitness are:
Selecting the proper student--When misbehavior occurs, teacher correctly
identifies the main culprit.
Attending to two or more misbehaviors simultaneously--The teacher correctly
directs and responds simultaneously to students working individually
and in groups.
Timing--The teacher does not allow misbehavior to spread to other students
before taking corrective action.

Momentum and Smoothness in Teaching--refers to pacing, buildup, and culmination
of lessons
Momentum--getting activities started promptly, keeping them moving ahead, and
bringing them to good close or transition
Smoothness--absence of abrupt changes during lessons that disrupt students' thought or
work
Poor momentum or smoothness may be due to
Jerkiness--failure to move smoothly from one activity to another, or from one
concept to another
Slowdowns--delays that waste time both during instruction and between
activities

Group Alerting and Accountability--getting and holding student attention and active
        participation
    Alerting--includes (1) getting students' attention and (2) informing them quickly of
        what they are supposed to do. Examples:
            "All eyes on me."
            "I have a question for you. Who can . . .?"
            "Listen carefully as Susan reads. When you hear the riddle, raise your
                thumb."
    Accountability--holding each student responsible for active involvement in lessons by
        doing such things as
            Asking all students to write an answer, then calling on two to respond.
            Circulating and observing students at work.

Overlapping--the teacher attends to two or more issues at the same time, such as
        Conducting small group instruction while directing independent seatwork
        Directing work on various independent projects simultaneously
        Correcting misbehavior in one part of the room while working in another

Valence and Challenge Arousal--Maintaining student interest)
        Positive techniques--adding excitements, richness to lessons: e.g.,"I've brought
            something special for you today."
        Negative techniques (to be avoided)--needless dwelling on matters or repeating
            directions, leaving students uninspired
        Challenge--statements during lessons such as "I bet nobody can get this one" or
            "Want to try something that's really hard?"
        Variety--varying activities, materials, groupings, and teacher roles, to spark
        interest and give relief from the usual listening, reading, and writing
        Progress--evidence of progress in learning, best depicted in graphs, charts, and
            time lines

The Ripple Effect

Withitness

Momentum and Smoothness in Teaching

Group Alerting and Accountability

Overlapping

Maintaining Student Interest

SUGGESTED INSTRUCTIONAL ACTIVITIES

Assignment

1. Read the chapter and do Application exercises as directed.

2. Make entries in the notebook for later use.

Short quiz on chapter contents.

Discussion Topics

1. How do you think the Kounin model compares with the Neo-Skinnerian model with regard to similarities, differences, and overall value?

2. What advantage might result from merging the Kounin and the Neo-Skinnerian models into one?

3. Kounin says that good lesson management is more powerful in affecting student behavior than any other discipline technique. To what extent do you think he might be right?

4. Have you ever had teachers who maintained control mostly by force of personality? Kounin implies that teacher personality has little to do with good discipline, that management skills are the key. Do you agree or disagree? Why?

5. On a scale of 1 to 5, with 5 the highest, how would you rate the Kounin model as concerns
- effectiveness?
- ease of implementation?
- personal appeal?
- major strengths?

6. Do you believe at this time that you would want to incorporate elements from the Kounin model into your own personal system of discipline? If so, what elements would you include, in order of importance?

Small-Group Collaborative Work

1. In groups of four or five, analyze Cases 2, 3, and 4 at the end of the chapter. Indicate how Kounin would have you deal with the situations depicted. Present your conclusions for class discussion.

2. Analyze Scenarios 3, 4, and 6 in Appendix I. Indicate how the Kounin model would be applied to those situations. Present your conclusions for discussion.

43

Guest Speaker

Invite a skilled teacher to discuss with the class specific lesson management techniques that he or she uses when teaching.

TEST ITEMS

The following pages provide test items related to the Kounin model. Answers are given here:

<u>True-False</u>: 1.T, 2.T, 3.F, 4.F, 5.F, 6.T, 7.T, 8.F, 9.F, 10.T, 11.F, 12.F, 13.T, 14.T, 15.T, 16.T, 17.F, 18.F, 19.F, 20.F

<u>Multiple Choice</u>: 1.a, 2.c, 3.a, 4.d, 5.b, 6.c, 7.a, 8.d, 9.b, 10.b, 11.d, 12.a, 13.d, 14.a, 15.c, 16.b, 17.a, 18.d, 19.a, 20.c

<u>Essay</u>:

1. Mostly learned, because they have to do with management (but partly related to personality and partly common-sense, too)
    Look for specific correct references to withitness, overlapping, movement management, and group focus.

2. A good short description is provided in "Comments on the Kounin Model" near end of chapter. It can be used as the criterion for judging student responses.

3. Accept the four specifics offered, if they are reasonable. Then judge the response in terms of the relation to Kounin's elements of progress, challenge, and variety. (Note the intentional mismatch between four specifics and three elements.)

4. Make sure Mr. Smith's work has challenge and variety; have him strive for better group focus; have him smooth out transitions so students get to work more quickly with less opportunity for goofing off; have Mr. Smith make better use of withitness and overlapping as he monitors his students at work.

Name_____Date_____

All items on this page relate to the KOUNIN model. Answer true or false as directed.

1. Classroom behavior depends largely on how teachers conduct their lessons.

2. Kounin's early investigations into classroom discipline focused on the ripple effect.

3. "Withitness" became the popularly used name for what Kounin meant by the ripple effect.

4. Withitness involves dividing the classroom into sections and focusing on each for a
    specified time.
5. Surprisingly, Kounin found transitions between lessons to have little effect on class
    behavior.
6. The ripple effect is more powerful at the elementary level than at the secondary level.

7. Withitness depends on ability to select the proper misbehaving student to receive a desist.

8. Clarity of a desist is more important to control than is quick selection of the correct culprit.

9. "Overlapping" is the term Kounin used to refer to transitions from one lesson to another.

10. Overlapping loses its effectiveness if the teacher does not also demonstrate withitness.

11. "Movement management" refers to organization of traffic patterns within the classroom.

12. "Slowdowns" are techniques used to slow teacher talk that is too rapid for students to
     follow.
13. Kounin found withitness, transitions, and momentum to be more powerful than other
     control techniques.
14. Kounin advocated grouping students so that a large percentage could be kept actively
     participating.
15. "Accountability" refers to each student's being responsible for what is taught in the lesson.

16. Accountability is usually increased when the teacher circulates and observes written
     responses.
17. Kounin advocated focusing on one student at a time as a means of increasing
     accountability.
18. Kounin found little relationship between behavior and the level of student attention during
     lessons.
19. "Satiation" in a lesson tends to produce higher levels of attention and achievement.

20. Providing variety in lesson activities is one step that is likely to increase satiation.

Name_____Date_____

All items relate to the KOUNIN model. Select the single best answer, as directed.

1. Amy is scolded; Sam straightens up. This is (a) ripple effect, (b) alerting, (c) focus, (d) clarity.
2. The least valuable quality of a desist is (a) clarity, (b) firmness, (c) roughness, (d) ripple.
3. The ripple effect is most powerful at (a) grade 1, (b) grade 7, (c) grade 11, (d) college level.
4. "Eyes in the back of the head" is like (a) focus, (b) overlapping, (c) accountability, (d) withitness.
5. Waiting for misbehavior to spread is a major error in (a) satiation, (b) timing, (c) alerting, (d) movement.
6. Which is most important in class control? (a) ripple effect, (b) clarity, (c) transitions, (d) format.
7. Overlapping loses its effectiveness without (a) withitness, (b) satiation, (c) format, (d) progress.
8. Selecting the correct student for a desist: (a) overlapping, (b) ripple, (c) focus, (d) withitness.
9. "Movement management" refers to (a) foot traffic, (b) lessons, (c) circulation, (d) distribution.
10. Most important to good control: (a) accountability, (b) transitions and momentum, (c) alerting, (d) ripple effect.
11. Least effective in delaying satiation is (a) progress, (b) challenge, (c) variety, (d) desists.
12. Satiation tends to produce increases in (a) errors, (b) attention, (c) achievement, (d) school enjoyment.
13. Group attention is increased most by (a) choosing a reciter before asking the question, (b) using a predictable response sequence, (c) focusing on one student at a time, (d) varying unison responses with individual responses.
14. Involvement is most damaged by (a) satiation, (b) ripple effect, (c) incorrect responses, (d) desists.
15. Dealing with more than one issue at a time: (a) rippling, (b) focusing, (c) overlapping, (d) spicing.
16. Movement management is concerned with (a) homework, (b) lessons, (c) taking turns, (d) entering and exiting the room.
17. Alerting and accountability are keys in (a) group focus, (b) restructuring, (c) overlapping, (d) format.
18. The Kounin model emphasizes teacher (a) personality, (b) creativity, (c) spontaneity, (d) lesson management.
19. Kounin's techniques are most helpful in misbehavior (a) prevention, (b) correction, (c) understanding, (d) documentation.
20. Kounin implies that control skills are (a) inborn, (b) idiosyncratic, (c) learned, (d) just common sense.

46

ESSAY EXAM: Write out your responses to the following items, as directed.

1. To what extent does Kounin suggest that discipline skills are learned, as distinct from inborn or derived from common sense? Support your conclusions with examples from withitness, overlapping, movement management, and group focus.

2. In no more than 100 words, provide your best description of the Kounin model. Use common words, avoiding special terms such as withitness, overlapping, satiation, and so forth.

3. Describe four specific things you would do to reduce boredom in the classes you teach. Indicate how your suggestions correspond to, or differ from, those provided by Kounin.

4. Mr. Smith teaches a class that contains many bright students who are poor at getting started on work and even worse at completing it. He scolds them constantly for laziness and horseplay. What suggestions would Kounin make to help Mr. Smith improve the behavior of his class?

Chapter 4

THE GINOTT MODEL
Discipline through Congruent Communication

CHAPTER ABSTRACT

Haim Ginott, a professor of psychology and psychiatry, wrote three acclaimed books on improving relationships between adults and youth: Between Parent and Child (1965), Between Parent and Teenager (1969), and Teacher and Child (1971). All three focused on detecting and correcting communication breakdowns that occur when adults speak to children and adolescents in ways that stifle communication, harm self-esteem, and cause resentment and hostility.

In his last book, Ginott had much to say about school discipline. He saw discipline not as a squelching technique invoked out of desperation but rather as an ongoing process that produces "a series of little victories," through which students gradually learn to assume responsibility for proper behavior.

The fundamental concept Ginott promoted had to do with what he called "sane messages"--messages that address problem situations while carefully avoiding any attack on the child's character or the attachment to it of any label (e.g., lazy, careless). When problems present themselves, teachers should simply address the situation ("It is too noisy") and indicate what is needed to correct the problem ("We need quiet in order to complete our work").

To obtain good behavior through this approach, teachers must do three additional things: (1) show good self-discipline in their own behavior, modeling what they want to see in their students; (2) use "congruent communication" that recognizes and acknowledges students' feelings about situations; and (3) invite cooperation rather than demand it.

Ginott allowed teachers to express displeasure strongly but urged that they use "I-messages" ("I am angry"; "I am appalled"). Even when upset, teachers should always remain helpful and humane so that students will want to learn in the classroom rather than rebel. As he wrote in Teacher and Child (New York: Avon, 1975), "A teacher's response has crucial consequences. It creates a climate of compliance or defiance, a mood of contentment or contention, a desire to make amends or to take revenge. It affects the child's conduct and character for better or for worse. Learning is always in the present tense, and it is always personal" (p. 34).

TERMINOLOGY

Sane messages--teacher messages to students that address the situation rather than attacking students' character; such messages do not blame, preach, command, accuse, belittle, or threaten.

I-messages--teacher messages to students in which teachers assess the situation and tell how they feel ("I am disappointed that . . . "I am unhappy about the . . . "I am unable to do my work").

48

Congruent communication--an authentic way of talking with students in which teacher comments match student feelings about situations

Inviting cooperation--telling students it is time for a certain activity, or giving them choices, as opposed to ordering, bossing, and commanding (which produce hostility and resistance)

Accepting feelings--acknowledging students' feelings of frustration, boredom, rejection, and so forth and then offering to be helpful instead of arguing against students' perceptions or denying them ("I can see that you are hurt by what was said.")

Labeling as disabling--harming students' self-perception and motivation through attaching labels (lazy, disrespectful, brilliant); students begin to feel that they must live up to the labels.

Correcting by directing--correcting student misbehavior not by scolding but by reiterating what should be done instead ("This is quiet study time")

Perils of sarcasm--students are often hurt by sarcasm. It is not to be used.

Perils of praise--because praise is judgmental, it manipulates students' feelings about themselves and creates dependence on others for approval and validation of the self. When used it should focus on work or behavior ("I'm delighted to see how much work you have accomplished"), not on students' character ("You are an exceptional student").

Inviting cooperation--asking students to do what is expected rather than trying to force them to do so through ordering, threatening, or preaching.

Being brief--teachers' making their point with very few words--what Ginott called "laconic language" ("We do not swear in this room").

Teachers expressing feelings--teachers are encouraged to express feelings, but through I-messages that do not label or attack students ("I am very angry about this situation").

APPRAISAL OF THE GINOTT MODEL

The major strength of the Ginott model is its guidance on how to talk with students so that they want to behave properly. It helps teachers avoid preaching and finding fault (which produce hostility and resistance) while accepting students' feelings and providing personal help. Teachers able to do this are often revered by students, who try in turn to cooperate.

For all its value, however, the Ginott model has two major shortcomings. First, it is slow-working. Even when its suggestions are fully implemented, misbehavior will continue to occur, at least for a time. Second, it provides no powerful techniques for suppressing serious misbehavior. The strongest step that Ginott suggests is the teacher's firm expression of anger or dismay through I-messages, a step that is effective only after the teacher has been able to gain the respect and support of the class.

INSTRUCTORS' DISCUSSION NOTES

Use Transparency 8 to guide discussion.

Ginott's Contributions to Classroom Discipline
  Emphasized making classrooms psychologically safe, humane, and helpful for students
  Showed importance of communication in building classroom discipline
  Explained nature and value of congruent communication
  Described communication of "teachers at their best"
  Described communication of "teachers at their worst"
  Encouraged teachers to express themselves genuinely but in ways that do not harm
       students

Discipline--A "series of little victories" teachers win through self-discipline and
         helpfulness, which promote cooperation and humaneness in students

Congruent Communication, Used by Teachers at Their Best
  Addresses situations, rather than character
  Invites cooperation   *Give, solicit examples of each
  Accepts and acknowledges feelings   of these congruent communication
  Expresses anger appropriately   situations.
  Uses brevity in correcting misbehavior
  Uses appreciative praise rather than evaluative praise

Noncongruent Communication, Used by Teachers at Their Worst
  Labels students and name-calls
  Asks rhetorical "whys" and gives moralistic lectures   *Give, solicit examples of each
  Invades students' privacy   of these noncongruent
  Makes caustic remarks to students   communication situations.
  Attacks students' character
  Demands, rather than invites, cooperation
  Denies students' feelings
  Shows loss of temper
  Uses evaluative praise to manipulate students

Ginott's Special Techniques
　　To correct student misbehavior--Use "laconic language" and show students how to behave
　　To express anger--Do so genuinely, but with no sarcasm or hostility
　　To praise students--Show appreciation for what students DO, not for what they are
　　To invite cooperation--Indicate what needs to be done, without bossing
　　To use hidden asset--Ask, "How can I be helpful to my students right now?"

SUGGESTED INSTRUCTIONAL ACTIVITIES

Assignment Read chapter, make entries into notebook, and complete application exercises as directed.

Quiz over the assigned reading.

Discussion Topics

1. Some critics say Ginott's suggestions are out of touch with the real world of today's classrooms, that students will scoff at teachers who act as Ginott suggests. What is your opinion in that regard?

2. Have you ever had a teacher who treated students as Ginott suggests? If so, how did you react at the time? What is your feeling toward that teacher now?

3. Ginott's suggestions concerning sane messages, I-messages, the use of praise, and correction as direction are contrary to most people's experience and inclination. How can his suggestions be implemented naturally? Do you think it reasonable that teachers be urged to learn his techniques?

4. How could Ginott's suggestions be incorporated into one of the previous models (Redl and Wattenberg, Kounin, Neo-Skinnerian) such that the selected model would be significantly improved?

5. To what extent do you believe your own teaching will be influenced by Ginott's suggestions? Explain.

6. Debate Topic: The Ginott model is more an overall approach to teaching than a system of discipline.

Small Group Collaborative Work

1. Analyze Cases 2 and 3 at the end of the chapter. How would Ginott suggest dealing with Sara and Joshua?

HAIM GINOTT ON DISCIPLINE

Discipline

Congruent Communication, Used by Teachers at Their Best

Noncongruent Communication, Used by Teachers at Their Worst

Ginott's Special Techniques

2. Locate the section in the textbook where Ginott describes teachers who use inappropriate discipline and those who use appropriate discipline. Select four behaviors from the improper list that have counterparts in the proper list. Expand them into short scenarios, then role-play them. For contrast, role-play their proper counterparts. Share with the entire class.

3. Turn to the list that describes teachers using proper discipline. Expand each behavior into a short scenario and take turns playing the teacher role. This is especially important, as it is the best way to make good responses come automatically.

4. Quickly review the scenarios in Appendix I and select two that you find most interesting. Decide how Ginott would have teachers deal with the situations.

TEST ITEMS

The following pages present true-false, multiple choice, and essay test items. Permission is granted for duplicating the items for class use. Answers are:

True-False: 1.T, 2.T, 3.T, 4.F, 5.F, 6.F, 7.T, 8.F, 9.F, 10.F, 11.T, 12.F, 13.T, 14.T, 15.F, 16.F, 17.T, 18.F, 19.T, 20.F

Multiple Choice: 1.a, 2.b, 3.b, 4.d, 5.d, 6.b, 7.c, 8.a, 9.d, 10.a, 11.b, 12.c, 13.b, 14.a, 15.b, 16.a, 17.a, 18.d, 19.c, 20.a.

Essay:
1. (a) sane message - communication that addresses a problem situation and indicates what needs to be done in order to correct it, without preaching, blaming, attacking, or labeling the student.
   (b) congruent communication - communication that recognizes and acknowledges students' feelings.   (c) "correcting as directing" - correcting improper student behavior not by scolding but by indicating an acceptable alternative.

2. (a) Ginott attempts to influence behavior through kindness, consideration, suggestion, example, and protection against feelings of hurt. The Neo-Skinnerians attempt to influence behavior by shaping it in desired directions through the use of reward (reinforcement).
   (b) Ginott attempts to correct misbehavior through the use of I-messages (to indicate disapproval) and suggestions on how to behave properly. The Neo-Skinnerians attempt to correct misbehavior through ignoring, reinforcing simultaneous "good" behavior, and punishment (as a last resort).
   (c) Behavior modification is the more popular for two reasons: (1) student behavior can be shaped with greater certainty through reinforcement than through sensitive communication and (2) procedures of behavior modification have a history of extensive use through a wide range of application.

3. Jonathan's teacher should briefly describe the situation to Jonathan, invite his cooperation, make sure not to label or criticize him, use I-messages to show displeasure, focus on solutions (suggest better behaviors), and remain helpful to Jonathan.

Name_____ Date_____

TRUE-FALSE. All items relate to the GINOTT model. Mark each item as directed.

1. The most important ingredient of classroom discipline is the teacher's own self-discipline.

2. Sane messages address the situation, not the student's character.

3. Praise and sarcasm both present areas of danger in communicating with students.

4. "Congruent communication" is defined as teachers' modeling the behavior they want to see in their students.

5. Teachers at their best find laudatory labels to apply to their students.

6. Ginott cautions teachers against expressing their own anger when upset.

7. Teachers should accept students' feelings of inferiority even when those feelings are clearly wrong.

8. "Correcting is directing" means clearly telling students what to do before they misbehave.

9. Sane messages describe what has upset the teacher and point out students' shortcomings in that regard.

10. Ginott says it is all right for teachers to lose their temper and self-control; such is only human.

11. Teacher responses should not contradict a student's perception of himself or herself.

12. Teachers, when expressing anger, should try to balance their use of I-messages with corresponding you-messages.

13. Saying "It is now work time" is a suggested way of inviting cooperation.

14. When students complain about treatment from others, teachers should ask, "How can I help you?"

15. Students fearful of speaking in front of the class should be reassured that they have no reason to be afraid.

16. Sarcasm is advocated for use in relieving tension, provided the teacher explains that it is only done in fun.

17. A main danger of praise is that it can manipulate students' feelings about themselves.

18. When students misbehave, the teacher should calmly ask, "Why are you doing that?"

19. Teachers should always show civilized behavior, even when students do not.

20. As a way to improve understanding, teachers should try to argue through disagreements with students.

Name_____ Date_____

Multiple choice. All items refer to the GINOTT model. Mark the single best response, as directed.

1. Ginott implied good discipline could normally be established (a) slowly, (b) sporadically, (c) quickly, (d) immediately.
2. Sane messages address (a) students' qualities, (b) situations, (c) cause-effect, (d) argumentation.
3. Congruent communication attends to (a) rules, (b) feelings, (c) directions, (d) assignments.

4. To guide desired behavior, the teacher should (a) praise, (b) reinforce, (c) admonish, (d) model.
5. To be avoided in the classroom: (a) anger, (b) sense of inferiority, (c) praise, (d) sarcasm.

6. Congruent communication most affects (a) homework, (b) self-esteem, (c) parental support, (d) apologies.
7. Regarding students, teachers should not (a) correct, (b) encourage, (c) label, (d) accept erroneous feelings of self-worth.
8. "This is quiet time": (a) sane message, (b) denial, (c) acceptance of feelings, (d) you-message.
9. In expressing anger, teachers should use (a) humor, (b) sarcasm, (c) you-messages, (d) I-messages.
10. Teacher behavior should always be (a) genuine, (b) neutral, (c) accepting, (d) cautious.

11. Inviting cooperation reduces student (a) apathy, (b) dependency, (c) self-assurance, (d) willingness.
12. Teachers, accepting feelings, should be (a) guides, (b) intermediaries, (c) sounding boards, (d) impartial judges.
13. Irrational student fears should be (a) interpreted, (b) accepted, (c) explained away, (d) disregarded.
14. Teacher labels students? (a) should not, (b) okay if positive, (c) okay if secret, (d) okay if student agrees.
15. The danger in praise: it manipulates one's feelings about (a) pain, (b) self, (c) danger, (d) pleasure.
16. Good discipline increases (a) will to learn, (b) conviviality, (c) irresponsibility, (d) temerity.
17. Threat of punishment produces (a) ill will, (b) desire to learn, (c) gentility, (d) compassion.
18. The teacher's main job is to provide an environment conducive to (a) good will, (b) cooperation, (c) mental health, (d) learning.
19. The Ginott model places major emphasis on (a) rule setting, (b) enforcement, (c) student responsibility, (d) hostility.
20. The Ginott model is weak concerning (a) enforcement, (b) responsibility, (c) humaneness, (d) teacher persistence.

ESSAY EXAM. Write out your responses to the following items, as directed.

1. Explain what Ginott meant by the following:
    (a) sane message
    (b) congruent communication
    (c) correcting as directing

2. Contrast Ginott's approach to classroom discipline with that advocated by the Neo-Skinnerians (behavior modification), by explaining:
    (a) how each attempts to influence behavior
    (b) how each attempts to correct misbehavior
    (c) why the Neo-Skinnerian approach is more widely used than is Ginott's approach.

3. Jonathan begins sixth grade with the following behaviors: talks without permission, swears, wastes time, and fails to complete assigned work. What would Ginott want Jonathan's teacher to do for the boy?

Chapter 5

THE DREIKURS MODEL
Discipline through Democratic Teaching and Confronting Mistaken Goals

CHAPTER ABSTRACT

Rudolf Dreikurs was born in Austria and trained there in psychiatry. After immigrating to the United States he specialized in family and child counseling. His interest in child behavior led to his writing extensively about behavior in classroom settings. Two of his most widely read books are Discipline Without Tears (1972) and Maintaining Sanity in the Classroom (1982).

He concluded that all students strive toward the genuine goal of belonging. Misbehavior results when students are frustrated in their attempts to reach that goal.

When thus frustrated, students turn to "mistaken goals," believing that those goals will bring what they want. The mistaken goals are (1) attention getting, (2) power seeking, (3) revenge seeking, and (4) displaying inadequacy. Students typically (though not always) pursue those goals in the order indicated; that is, first they try attention getting (and if it does not work) then power (and if that does not work) then revenge (and if that does not work) then displays of inadequacy.

Dreikurs firmly asserted that teachers must not think of discipline as punishment; rather, they must see it as a process of teaching students to impose limits on themselves.

To assist this process, teachers should see to it that all students receive recognition and feel they belong. While they are learning to set limits on themselves, students must live by rules of classroom behavior that are linked to consequences invoked when the rules are broken. Students are given a voice in establishing rules and consequences. When misbehavior occurs that indicates a mistaken goal, teachers should confront students and make sure that the misbehavior is not reinforced. The type of mistaken goal can be recognized through the teacher's reaction: if the teacher is annoyed, the student's goal is attention-getting; if threatened, power-seeking; if hurt, seeking revenge; and if the teacher feels powerless, the student's goal is to display inadequacy.

Dreikurs used the term "democratic" in referring to his overall discipline scheme comprised of rules, consequences, guidance, teaching, and student involvement. He made a clear distinction between this democratic approach and those that are weakly ineffective ("permissive") or overly harsh ("autocratic"), both of which fail to teach self-discipline. Democratic discipline helps students learn that they are responsible for their actions and must respect themselves and others.

TERMINOLOGY

Discipline--teaching students to impose limits on themselves.

Autocratic teachers--teachers who force their will on students to prove they have control of the classroom.

57

Permissive teachers--teachers who fail to provide standards and guidance through a system of humane rules and consequences.

Democratic teachers--teachers who provide guidance through rules and consequences while allowing students to participate in decision making.

Democratic classrooms--classrooms in which teachers and students make joint decisions regarding procedures, rules, and consequences.

Genuine goal of belonging--students' prime goal of feeling a sense of belonging in the class.

Mistaken goals--goals toward which students direct behavior when frustrated in their attempts to gain belonging and recognition, believing the mistaken goals will bring them what they want.

Attention getting--a mistaken goal; the student tries through misbehavior to get attention from the teacher and classmates.

Power seeking--a mistaken goal; the student confronts the teacher in a power struggle, usually after failing to obtain the attention desired.

Revenge seeking--a mistaken goal; the student, unsuccessful in a power struggle with the teacher, attempts to get revenge by hurting the teacher.

Displaying inadequacy--a mistaken goal; the student who has failed to find gratification through attention, power, or revenge seeking, plays stupid and helpless, making no effort to participate.

Encouragement--words or actions that convey the teacher's respect for and belief in students' abilities (used as an alternative for praise, which Dreikurs believed dangerous).

Praise--recognition given for tasks or behavior (to be avoided, Dreikurs says, because it promotes the idea that a product or behavior is worthless unless praised).

Logical consequences--unpleasant consequences (not physical punishment) invariably invoked when a rule is broken (called "logical" because of their connection with the misbehavior; e.g., when work is not done during study time, the student must stay after class to finish it).

APPRAISAL OF THE DREIKURS MODEL

The Dreikurs model has two significant strengths. The first is its ability to help students reach their primary goal of belonging in the classroom, thus eliminating much of the mistaken-goal behavior that causes discipline problems. The second is even more important. Dreikurs' suggestions concerning teaching students to respect others and take responsibility for their own actions can, over time, cause students to behave well because they realize that doing so is best for themselves and others. In short, they behave well because they want to, not because they are forced.

Despite these strengths, many teachers are uncomfortable about spending so much time in talking (counseling) with students about behavior, which cuts into precious instructional time. Too, they find fault in the model's relative lack of clear-cut guidance on how exactly to suppress misbehavior. Dreikurs says to confront mistaken goals by asking, "Could it be that you want me to pay more attention to you?" or "Could it be that you want to hurt me?" Dreikurs also emphasizes the invocation of logical consequences when rules are broken. But teachers want to know more about how to make those consequences effective and what exactly to do when students defy them or when contagious misbehavior breaks out.

The Dreikurs model, then, is rather strong in the preventive facet of discipline. It is adequate in the corrective facet as well for classes that are relatively well behaved. But for building long-term good behavior, the model has great potential for developing in students a genuine desire to behave acceptably, out of respect for themselves and others.

INSTRUCTORS' DISCUSSION NOTES

Use Transparency 9 to guide discussion.

Dreikurs's Contributions to Classroom Discipline
    The relationship between sense of belonging and classroom behavior
    The nature and importance of democratic teaching
    The genuine goal of belonging and the mistaken goals of attention,
        power, revenge, and displaying inadequacy
    The use of encouragement and logical consequences instead of
        punishment in correcting misbehavior

Classroom Discipline, According to Dreikurs
    Undesirable--Aversive control and punishment imposed on students,
        usually by autocratic teachers. Or in contrast, lack of control where students are
        irresponsibly allowed to do as they please.
    Desirable--Self-discipline in which students regulate their own behavior.
        This is most often accomplished by democratic teachers.
    How Good Discipline is Attained--Good discipline is attained by helping
        students acquire a sense of belonging, through (1) democratic teaching and (2)
        confronting mistaken goals.

Democratic Teaching--Friendly teachers establish order necessary for learning, invite
        students to cooperate, provide stimulation, encourage sharing of ideas, provide
        direction and guidance, share responsibility, acknowledge students and their work,
        and involve students in making decisions that affect the class.

Autocratic teaching--teachers lay down the law in the classroom, allow little student input, boss students around, exert pressure, demand cooperation, make all rules and consequences unilaterally, find fault, criticize, and dominate. Examples . . .
Permissive teaching--teachers put few limits on students, allow students to do much as they wish, accept whatever students do, and fail to help students understand that freedom must be linked to responsible behavior. Examples . . .

Goals of Student Behavior
    Genuine Goal--toward which much classroom behavior is aimed:
        Belonging--All students want to feel they belong, to the group, the class, the school. They do not want to feel isolated, left out, unnoticed, not a part of things. A great majority of student behavior is efforts expended in trying to belong.
    Mistaken Goals--what students seek when unable to obtain a sense of belonging
        Attention Getting--do things, usually unacceptable, to get attention from the teacher and others. If that does not succeed, they next try . . .
        Power seeking--struggle against the teacher, usually by refusing to do what is asked or demanded of them. If that does not succeed, they next try . . .
        Revenge Seeking--try to get revenge on the teacher by defacing property, cheating, or spreading lies. If that does not succeed, they next try . . .
        Displaying inadequacy--withdraw from class and lessons, making no attempt to participate and rejecting teacher offers to help
    Misbehavior is often a manifestation of students' pursuing mistaken goals.

Identifying Mistaken Goals: If student misbehavior makes teacher feel
        Annoyed--then the mistaken goal is probably "attention getting."
        Threatened--then the mistaken goal is probably "power seeking."
        Hurt--then the mistaken goal is probably "seeking revenge."
        Powerless--then the mistaken goal is probably "displaying inadequacy."

Control Techniques for When Students Misbehave
    Undesirable:
        Punishment
        Humiliation or isolation imposed by the teacher.
    Desirable:
        Logical Consequences--Reasonable results that follow good and bad behavior
        Encouragement--Words and actions that convey teacher belief in students' abilities.
        Confronting Mistaken Goals--Questioning students directly about the possible goal of their behavior. (give examples:)

RUDOLF DREIKURS ON DISCIPLINE

Classroom Discipline

Styles of Teaching

Goals of Student Behavior

Identifying Mistaken Goals

Control Techniques for When Students Misbehave

SUGGESTED INSTRUCTIONAL ACTIVITIES

Assignment

1. Read the chapter and make entries into notebook.

2. Complete application exercises at end of chapter, as directed.

Quiz over chapter contents.

Discussion Questions

1. Briefly, what is your overall impression of the Dreikurs model? (Follow-up questions: What do you think of its major goal of responsible behavior? Can the goal be reached by the typical teacher? That is, could you, for example, implement the model effectively? What do you like best about the model? What leaves you uneasy?)

2. What similarities do you see between the Dreikurs model and that of Redl and Wattenberg? (Ans: Both attend to motives within students [a psychoanalytic orientation], view misbehavior as related to the social setting of the classroom, advocate rules and consequences, and emphasize encouragement.) Do you see a similar compatibility between the Dreikurs model and those of Kounin and Ginott?

3. What do you think would be the likely result of your asking mistaken-goal questions as Dreikurs suggests (e.g., "Could it be that you want to prove that nobody can make you do anything?" "Could it be that you want to hurt me and others?")

4. Again we see an authority cautioning against the use of praise. Ginott said not to praise, now Dreikurs concurs. Yet teachers everywhere use praise all the time; obviously they believe in doing so. How do you reconcile this disagreement between advice and practice? Or is the difference only one of semantics?

Small-Group Collaborative Work

1. Analyze Cases 2, 3, and 4 (Sara, Joshua, Tom) and decide what Dreikurs would suggest. Present to class for discussion.

2. From Appendix I in the text, analyze Scenarios 1, 2, 6, and 9. Present conclusions to class for discussion.

TEST ITEMS

The following pages present true-false, multiple choice, and essay exam items. Permission is granted to reproduce the items for classroom use.

Answers

True-False: 1.F, 2.F, 3.F, 4.F, 5.T, 6.T, 7.T, 8.F, 9.T, 10.F, 11.T, 12.T, 13.T, 14.T, 15.F, 16.F, 17.T, 18.F, 19.T, 20.T

Multiple Choice: 1.d, 2.b, 3.d, 4.a, 5.a, 6.c, 7.b, 8.a, 9.a, 10.a, 11.b, 12.d, 13.b, 14.b, 15.d, 16.d, 17.b, 18.b, 19.c, 20.a

Essay

1. Dreikurs was explaining styles of teaching and classroom organization that affect (promote or inhibit) good discipline. "Permissives" do not provide the guidance and limits that students need. "Autocrats" are too harshly controlling and do not allow freedom of behavior coupled with logical consequences that lead to self-discipline. "Democratic" teachers explain to students the need for rules and limits, involve students in establishing both, and allow choice of behavior (together with the consequences attached to it).

2. (a) Attention seeking--behavior intended to draw attention of teacher and other students, used when a student does not feel adequate sense of personal significance or belonging to the class.

Power seeking--the second mistaken goal, in which students feel they can gain personal significance through resisting teacher requests.

Revenge seeking--the third mistaken goal, in which students feel they can gain, through hurting the teacher, the significance they have not gained through attention-seeking or power-seeking.

Displaying inadequacy--the fourth mistaken goal, in which students attempt to protect a fragile sense of self-importance through refusal to work or cooperate.

(b) Teachers are advised first to do everything possible to see that all students feel that they belong in the class and are recognized as important to it. Beyond that, teachers are to confront mistaken-goal behavior, point it out, and explain the faulty logic on which it is based. Example: "Can it be that you want people to pay attention to you? Everyone likes attention and wants to feel important. Let's all keep that in mind. Meanwhile, remember that the best way to get attention and feel important is through doing good work and being a good friend to classmates."

3. Mistaken-goal behavior is identified in two ways. The first is through analysis of student behavior, as follows:
    -If student misbehaves, stops, then repeats misbehavior, the goal is attention getting.
    -If student misbehaves and refuses to stop, the goal is power seeking.
    -If student becomes hostile or violent, the goal is revenge seeking.
    -If the student refuses to participate or cooperate, the goal is displaying inadequacy.

The second way to identify mistaken-goal behavior is through the teacher's reaction to misbehavior, as follows:
    -If the teacher is annoyed, the student's goal is attention getting.

-If the teacher's authority is threatened, the student's goal is power seeking.
-If the teacher's feelings are hurt, the student's goal is revenge seeking.
-If the teacher feels powerless, the student's goal is displaying inadequacy.

4. (a) Dreikurs saw <u>encouragement</u> as teacher words and actions that indicate respect for students and belief in their abilities. Encouragement recognizes effort and improvement, not achievement. It accepts students as they are, not just as they "should be."

<u>Praise</u> on the other hand is given as evaluation of a product completed or as an appraisal of student character. It promotes the idea that nothing is of value unless praised.

(b) Examples of encouragement: "I can tell that you have really been trying hard." "You seem to enjoy this work."
Examples of praise: "You are really a smart girl!" "Your artwork is fantastic!"

(c) Dreikurs valued encouragement highly. He believed it drew on inner motivation, promoted effort, and allowed students to judge themselves. For Dreikurs, praise had the opposite effect. It drew on motivation from sources outside the student, taught that nothing is worthwhile unless praised, and took self-judgment away from students.

5. Dreikurs' "don'ts" are not the same as logical consequences. The "don'ts" tell teachers what they <u>should not do</u> when teaching. Logical consequences, on the other hand, are penalties imposed on students when they choose to break rules. Students have a say in establishing rules and consequences, understand them, and know that consequences will always be invoked when rules are broken.

ESSAY EXAM. Write out your answers to the following items as directed.

1. What was Dreikurs getting at in contrasting permissive teachers, autocratic teachers, and democratic teachers, as concerns discipline?

2. (a) Describe the mistaken goals clarified by Dreikurs and (b) explain how teachers are supposed to deal with them in the classroom.

3. How is mistaken-goal behavior in students identified? Be specific.

4. (a) Explain the distinction Dreikurs made between encouragement and praise. (b) Give two examples of each. (c) Why did he value one over the other?

5. Dreikurs presented teachers a number of "don'ts"--don't scold, nag, use threats, find fault with students, ask students to promise anything, and so forth. Are these don'ts the same as logical consequences? Explain.

Name_____ Date_____

All items relate to the DREIKURS model. Answer true or false, as directed.

1. Discipline and punishment are different names for what is essentially the same process.

2. Autocratic discipline gives students a primary role in deciding on rules, consequences, and enforcement.
3. Displaying inadequacy is the students' first mistaken goal.

4. Teachers should praise students' work but not their character.

5. Power seeking is the second of students' four mistaken goals.

6. Good discipline has little to do with punishment, as punishment suggests humiliation and revenge.
7. Good discipline requires freedom of choice for students and understanding of consequences.
8. Consequences for breaking rules should be invoked intermittently so as to keep students on guard.
9. Students have the responsibility to influence their classmates to behave appropriately.

10. Students in permissive classrooms are most likely to learn how society really functions.

11. According to Dreikurs, students want guidance and leadership.

12. Good discipline helps students choose the behaviors that get them what they want.

13. Democratic teachers allow students freedom to choose their own behavior.

14. Democratic teachers teach students they must invariably suffer the consequences of their misbehavior.
15. Teachers should give attention to misbehaving students in order to show that they really care.
16. Revenge seeking enables students to find acceptance through hurting others.

17. Teachers should try to identify the mistaken goal when a student misbehaves.

18. If a student stops a misbehavior, then soon repeats it, the mistaken goal is "displaying inadequacy."
19. Teachers should confront students with the faulty logic upon which mistaken goals are based.
20. Teachers should at first ignore students' undue bids for attention.

Name_____ Date_____

Multiple Choice. All items relate to the DREIKURS model. Mark the single best answer, as directed.

1. Discipline is best described as (a) belonging, (b) punishment, (c) reinforcement, (d) limit setting.
2. Good discipline must involve (a) authority, (b) choice, (c) permissiveness, (d) mistaken goals.
3. Which contributes least to a democratic classroom? (a) order, (b) limits, (c) leadership, (d) praise.
4. Freedom is most likely to grow from (a) discipline, (b) reinforcement, (c) permissiveness, (d) belonging.
5. A democratic classroom emphasizes (a) cooperation, (b) competition, (c) praise, (d) student promises.
6. Sammy misbehaves, stops, then misbehaves again. He is probably seeking (a) power, (b) revenge, (c) attention, (d) inadequacy.
7. Alice's behavior hurts the teacher's feelings. Alice is probably seeking (a) power, (b) revenge, (c) attention, (d) inadequacy.
8. Students follow mistaken goals believing they will gain personal (a) significance, (b) growth, (c) freedom, (d) admiration.
9. Students who display inadequacy pretend they are (a) stupid, (b) smart, (c) caring, (d) responsible.
10. Student seeks mistaken goal; teacher should confront faulty (a) logic, (b) pride, (c) psyche, (d) fear.
11. Student engages teacher in power struggle; teacher should (a) give in, (b) withdraw, (c) fight back, (d) invoke punishment.
12. Students who display inadequacy are frequently overly (a) cautious, (b) fearful, (c) animated, (d) ambitious.
13. Teachers make learning seem worthwhile through (a) competition, (b) encouragement, (c) praise, (d) wit.
14. Internal motivation is increased by (a) praise, (b) encouragement, (c) permissiveness, (d) freedom.
15. "Your work has improved!" is an example of (a) praise, (b) reality, (c) criticism, (d) encouragement.
16. Logical consequences are (a) mild threats, (b) mild punishers, (c) negative reinforcers, (d) results.
17. Logical consequences: apply them (a) forcefully, (b) consistently, (c) intermittently, (d) smilingly.
18. Teachers should treat students as they would (a) emerging adults, (b) their social equals, (c) their own children, (d) innately wiser than adults.
19. The Dreikurs model is strong in (a) improving behavior quickly, (b) suppressing misbehavior, (c) promoting lasting improvement, (d) requiring firm limits.
20. The Dreikurs model is weakest in (a) squelching misbehavior, (b) building trust, (c) invoking consequences, (d) promoting a sense of responsibility.

Chapter 6

THE CANTER MODEL
Discipline through Assertively Managing Behavior

CHAPTER ABSTRACT

Lee Canter, a specialist in child guidance, believes that almost all students are capable of behaving well and that when they do not it is because they either enjoy misbehaving or do not understand how they are supposed to behave in particular situations.

In his Assertive Discipline, Canter tries to help teachers take charge responsibly in the classroom so as to meet needs humanely. Students need and want limits on behavior, he says, and have a right to receive good instruction in an environment that is accepting and helpful. Teachers also have rights to which they are entitled--to teach as they judge best in an environment free from disruption and threat while receiving backing from administrators and parents.

Canter believes that in order to enjoy those student and teacher rights, teachers need to implement a system of discipline that is effective, efficient, and nonconfrontive.

In the early 1970s Canter, assisted by his wife, Marlene, began developing and testing discipline techniques that enabled teachers to maintain control without having to engage in frustrating, time-wasting confrontations. In 1976 he published Assertive Discipline: A Take-Charge Approach for Today's Educator, in which he advocated a discipline system that established rules and consequences that teachers could enforce easily and humanely. That approach became enormously popular. As time passed, Canter modified it somewhat to emphasize directly teaching students how they are expected to behave in various situations.

Assertive Discipline is comprised of elements seen in earlier models of discipline, but Canter has made his model the most popular ever by attending to four fundamental considerations: First, he strongly maintains that teachers and students both have rights in the classroom that are damaged by misbehavior; second, he insists that firm discipline, properly maintained, is humane and liberating for students; third, he stresses that students must be taught how they are expected to behave in the classroom; and fourth, he provides a clear, effective, and practical approach for implementing his ideas, one that makes sense to teachers.

Canter and his associates have continued to update their techniques and materials, as seen in Assertive Discipline Phase 2: In-Service Media Package (1986), Assertive Discipline for Secondary School Educators: In-Service Video Package and Leader's Manual (1989), Assertive Discipline: Positive Behavior Management for Today's Classrooms (1992), Succeeding with Difficult Students: New Strategies for Reaching Your Most Challenging Students (1993), and a variety of other materials to assist teachers in using Assertive Discipline and working with parents.

TERMINOLOGY

Students' needs--students need a concerned teacher who is able to set consistent limits on behavior while at the same time providing warmth, personal attention, and support.

Student rights--students have the right to teachers who work for students' best interests by placing limits on misbehavior while providing support and encouragement.

Teacher rights--teachers have the right to teach in a classroom free from disruption and supported by parents and administrators.

Limit setting--the process of making plain which behaviors are acceptable and unacceptable in the classroom.

Teaching good behavior--good behavior management requires that teachers not simply set limits but go well beyond that to actually teaching students how to behave in the classroom.

Positive recognition--the sincere, meaningful attention teachers give students who behave according to expectations.

Consequences--penalties teachers invoke when students violate class expectations. Consequences must be something students dislike (staying in after class, isolation from the group) but must never be physically or psychologically harmful.

Assertive teacher--a teacher who clearly and firmly communicates needs and requirements to students and follows those words with appropriate actions.

Roadblocks to Assertive Discipline--mistaken beliefs that inhibit teachers' establishing good classroom discipline.

Nonassertive responses--teacher responses that fail to back up violations of behavior standards with appropriate actions.

Hostile responses--teacher responses to misbehavior that attack and belittle students.

Assertive responses--teacher responses that continually help students comply with established expectations. Words are backed up principally with positive recognition. Consequences are invoked only when all else fails.

Positive repetitions--involve repeating directions as positive statements to students who are complying with class rules. For example: "Fred remembered to raise his hand. Good job."

Moving-in--a technique used when one or two chronically misbehaving students do not respond to normal consequences. It involves moving directly to the student, making eye contact, restating directions to be followed, and indicating what the next consequence will be for further misbehavior.

68

APPRAISAL OF THE CANTER MODEL

Assertive Discipline is far and away the most popular system of discipline used in American schools today, which gives testimony to its inherent strengths. To restate those strengths briefly, they include teachers' taking charge, insistence on students' rights and teachers' rights, insistence on cooperation and support from parents and administrators, teaching students how to behave responsibly in the classroom, an intervention technique that avoids most confrontations and preserves both teaching time and teacher equanimity, ability to enforce rules quickly, and even-handedness in application. All of these combine to yield Assertive Discipline's greatest strength--effectiveness--and that, of course, is why it is so enormously popular.

Assertive Discipline does not escape criticism, however, and it is not the preferred discipline system for all teachers, students, subjects, and grade levels. Among the criticisms it receives are the following: It is too rigid, too overwhelming, especially for very young children. Others say the system depends too much on externally applied restrictions (meaning that students do not as a result change behavior genuinely from the inside) and that it lacks ability to engender care and compassion within the group. The severest critics say that the system only shows once again that teachers have all the power and students have none.

Teachers who champion Assertive Discipline find little merit in those criticisms, insisting that the system makes classroom life and learning better for all concerned. They especially like its effectiveness in stopping misbehavior quickly, and they appreciate the fact that changes are continually made in program techniques and materials to keep them current with emerging needs and trends.

All in all, Assertive Discipline is the most powerful of all models when it comes to corrective discipline. Because students are taught how to behave and are made fully aware of rules and consequences, it is strong in preventive discipline as well.

INSTRUCTORS' DISCUSSION NOTES

Use Transparency 10 to guide discussion.

Canter's Contributions to Classroom Discipline
    Championed classroom "rights" of both students and teachers
    Showed teachers how to take charge in the classroom and exert positive control
    Emphasized the importance of actually teaching students how to behave properly
    Showed how to deal positively and effectively with classroom disruptions without
        losing teaching time

Rights in the Classroom
    Students' Rights
        To learn in a supportive, caring environment free from threat
        To be taught clearly how they are expected to behave
        To have reasonable limits on their behavior described and enforced
    Teachers' Rights
        To teach in an efficient learning environment free from disruptions
        To teach in ways that are consistent with teachers' strengths
        To receive backing from administrators and parents

Traits of Assertive Teachers
        Leaders in the classroom
        Clearly communicate expectations, support students, and follow through
        Care enough about themselves not to allow students to disrupt teaching
        Care enough about students not to allow them to behave in ways not
                in the students' best interests
        Specific actions include
                Specify expectations clearly
                Set and enforce desirable limits on student behavior
                Use hints and I-messages to request appropriate behavior
                Interact with students concerning appropriate behavior and why
                        rules are needed
                When misbehavior occurs, follow through with established
                        consequences rather than threats

Steps That Lead to Assertive Discipline
Recognize and Remove Roadblocks to Assertive Discipline, such as
Negative expectations about one's ability to deal with misbehavior
Negative expectations about one's ability to exert positive influence
Belief that one functions in isolation, without support from others
Practice Assertive Response Styles, differentiating among:
Nonassertive comments such as "Would you please try to stop that?"
Hostile comments such as "You either do that work, or you'll regret it!"
Assertive comments such as "It's against our rules to be discourteous; that's a
warning."
Make a Discipline Plan That Contains Clear Rules, Positive Recognitions, and
Effective Consequences. With the class:
Discuss examples of clear rules, e.g., "Always follow directions."
Discuss examples of positive recognition, e.g., "Thanks for raising your hand."
Discuss examples of effective consequences, e.g., "You have chosen to stay in
for two minutes after class is dismissed."
Teach the Discipline Plan to Students
Teach the plan, expectations, positive recognitions, and consequences through
explanation and discussion.
Teach Students How to Behave Responsibly
Demonstrate exactly how students are expected to behave and have them role-
play to show understanding and establish correct habits.

Dealing with Misbehavior
Nondisruptive Off-Task Behavior
No consequences need be invoked. Instead, make eye contact, use physical
proximity, say the student's name, or praise a nearby student who is
behaving properly.
Invoking consequences
Follow your plan calmly. Be consistent. Provide an escape mechanism,
such as allowing the student to write about the problem in a journal.
Give the offending student positive recognition as soon as the
opportunity arises.
Dealing with difficult students
For chronic offenders, use one-on-one problem solving conferences and
try to build positive relationships with the students by giving them
personal attention, spending time with them, and visiting them at home.

LEE CANTER ON DISCIPLINE

Rights in the Classroom

Traits of Assertive Teachers

Steps That Lead to Assertive Discipline

Dealing with Misbehavior

SUGGESTED INSTRUCTIONAL ACTIVITIES

Assignments

    1. Read assigned chapter and complete Application exercises as directed.
    2. Make entries into notebook.

Quiz over chapter contents.

Discussion Topics

1. Many people when first learning about the Canter model have the reaction that it is too strongly controlling of student behavior. What do you think of the model, all in all?

2. To what extent do you agree with Canter's premise that almost all students can behave properly, but often simply choose to misbehave?

3. What is your understanding of Canter's explanations of student and teacher "rights" in the classroom? Does his concept of classroom rights seem to you to be a valuable one for teachers?

4. Some readers consider Canter's depictions of hostile and nonassertive teachers to be overdone. Have you seen clear examples of each, and have you seen teachers similar to those he calls "assertive"? If so, what were your personal reactions to those teachers?

5. For the Canter model to work well, it must have the backing of the school administration and parental backing, too. How does Canter suggest ensuring that you have such backing?

6. Some critics consider Canter's system insufficiently humane. (Canter strongly disagrees with this criticism.) Could such criticism be softened if more elements from Ginott and Dreikurs were incorporated into Assertive Discipline, or would that render Canter's approach ineffective?

Small-Group Collaborative Work

1. Discuss Concept Cases 2, 3, and 4 in the Application exercises at the end of the chapter. Explain how Canter would have the teacher deal with each. Discuss with entire class.

2. Through role playing, take turns practicing nonassertive, hostile, and assertive responses to situations in which students (a) play too much during work time, (b) call out in discussions without raising hands, and (c) call others names in the classroom.

3. Pretend that Albert, an aggressively angry student, is calling you foul names in front of the class. When you invoke negative consequences, he increases the verbal aggression against you. Describe how you will deal with him. Take turns practicing your forceful, yet calm, responses.

4. Select one of the following Appendix I Scenarios 1, 2, 3, 8, 9, or 10. Decide how Canter would suggest dealing with the situation depicted. Present conclusions to the class.

TEST ITEMS

The following pages present true-false, multiple choice, and essay test items.

Answers

True-False: 1.T, 2.T, 3.T, 4.T, 5.F, 6.T, 7.F, 8.T, 9.T, 10.F, 11.F, 12.F, 13.F, 14.F, 15.T, 16.T, 17.T, 18.F, 19.F, 20.F

Multiple Choice: 1.c, 2.b, 3.a, 4.d, 5.a, 6.d, 7.b, 8.a, 9.b, 10.c, 11.a, 12.d, 13.a, 14.d, 15.c, 16.b, 17.c, 18.b, 19.b, 20.c

Essay
1. Yes. Without the presence of reward, Canter's system would probably still be effective, as students would behave properly out of fear of negative consequences. However, without reward (positive consequences), students would be likely to develop negative attitudes such as fear of teacher, dislike of schooling, and willingness to behave properly only when threatened.

2. Step 1: Recognize and remove roadblocks to Assertive Discipline, such as negative expectations about students' behavior and failure to recognize that teachers can have a positive influence on all students.
Step 2: Practice assertive response styles (firmly but unemotionally say what you mean and mean what you say, as contrasted with nonassertive and hostile styles).
Step 3: Make a discipline plan that contains good rules and clear, effective consequences such as
. . .
Step 4: Teach the discipline plan to students, by . . .
Step 5: Teach students how to behave responsibly in settings such as . . .

3. Special strengths include effectiveness, ease of application, the reemphasis of teacher and student rights in the classroom, the reduction of confrontations between teacher and students, the stress on students' choosing consequences through their behavior, and the saving of instructional time lost through most other approaches to discipline. Limitations in the view of many teachers are that it is too harsh, mechanical, demeaning, and overpowering for primary students.

Criteria for judging your students' personal reactions to the system might include their persuasiveness, logic, and use of specific examples.

4. The steps are (1) hold private one-on-one problem-solving conferences in which you express your concern and listen to those of the student; (2) use positive support (personal attention home visits, get-well cards) to build a positive relationship with the student; and (3) develop an individualized behavior plan that spells out the exact behaviors that are desired and what will happen when the student does and does not meet expectations.

Name_____ Date_____

All items pertain to the CANTER model. Answer each true or false, as directed.

1. Parents, generally speaking, support the intent of Assertive Discipline and the procedures it involves.
2. Firm control of student behavior, correctly maintained, is humane and liberating.

3. Students have the right to choose how they will behave in the classroom.

4. Assertive Discipline emphasizes teacher persistence in stating personal feelings and expectations.
5. Most misbehavior results from student problems beyond the control of the teacher.

6. Teachers are entitled to have their classroom needs met if students are not harmed as a result.
7. Most good teachers need not obtain backing from administrators; they can handle their own problems.
8. Teachers should respond to students in ways that help students comply with classroom rules.
9. A major roadblock to learning to use Assertive Discipline is negative expectations about students.
10. A fundamental principle of Assertive Discipline is its insistence on treating all students alike.
11. Assertive teachers tell students what they think of them in no uncertain terms.

12. Nonassertive teachers typically insist that students comply with class rules.

13. When students behave badly, teachers may properly invoke consequences that have not been explained in advance.
14. An assertive teacher might well say, "This makes five times I've told you; I'm getting sick of this."
15. Positive consequences are more important to good discipline than are negative consequences.
16. Canter's "positive consequences" are approximately the same thing as Skinner's "reinforcers."
17. In Assertive Discipline, teachers stress that no student will be allowed to break the rules.

18. Assertive teachers are expected to record student misbehaviors with names on the board.

19. Most teachers use "assertive response styles" naturally when dealing with student misbehavior.
20. An assertive teacher might well say, "Please try your very best not to call anyone names again."

Name_____ Date_____

All items relate to the CANTER model. Mark the single best answer, as directed.

1. Most failing teachers fail because they don't (a) teach well enough, (b) kiss
   up to principals, (c) have adequate discipline, (d) behave morally.
2. To request and expect appropriate behavior is a teacher (a) duty, (b) right, (c) illusion,
   (d) trap.
3. Assertive response styles are best learned through (a) practice, (b) reflection, (c) analysis,
   (d) recognition.
4. In Assertive Discipline, negative expectations about students are considered a (a) given,
   (b) right,   (c) response, (d) roadblock.
5. Not listed as a teacher response style is (a) benign, (b) hostile, (c) assertive,
   (d) nonassertive.
6. "Please try" suggests which response style? (a) benign, (b) hostile, (c) assertive,
   (d) nonassertive.
7. "Requesting appropriate behavior" may involve (a) shouts, (b) hints, (c) disputes,
   (d) bargaining.
8. "Delivering verbal limits" may involve (a) eye contact, (b) requests, (c) hints, (d) pleas.

9. Responsible classroom behavior should be (a) expected, (b) taught, (c) inferred,
   (d) transferred from home.
10. Working with very hard to manage students may require special (a) sternness,
    (b) demands on parents, (c) efforts to build relationships, (d) authority.
11. Positive statements about how students are to behave are called (a) limits,
    (b) consequences, (c) invocations, (d) follow-through.
12. Consequences most effective in discipline are (a) implied, (b) assigned, (c) neutral,
    (d) positive.
13. Consequences should be selected (a) in advance, (b) as the occasion warrants, (c) by
    students from a list, (d) by the administrator.
14. Special privilege is what type of consequence? (a) implied, (b) proactive, (c) quiet,
    (d) positive.
15. Canter's system is especially strong in which facet of discipline? (a) analytic,
    (b) supportive, (c) corrective, (d) reformative.
16. Primary teachers sometimes say Canter's system is too (a) lenient, (b) harsh,
    (c) democratic, (d) simple.
17. Teachers like Assertive Discipline because it reduces (a) teaching time, (b) student
    motivation, (c) confrontations, (d) administrator meddling.
18. Assertive Discipline does not work optimally unless supported by (a) community, (b)
    parents, (c) research, (d) the media.
19. Assertive Discipline clearly communicates (a) goal statements, (b) expectations,
    (c) probable outcomes, (d) the role of the community.
20. Assertive Discipline depends on consistency of (a) goal, (b) desist, (c) follow-through,
    (d) reprieve.

<u>Essay Exam</u>. Write out your answers to the following items, as directed.

1. Canter advocates the use of reward for good student behavior and assigns it importance in his system. Could Canter's system work without the presence of reward? Explain your answer.

2. Canter's work suggests that teachers can transform themselves into assertive teachers through a series of five steps. Identify the steps and describe what each entails.

3. Indicate what are generally considered to be the special strengths as well as the limitations of the Canter model. Explain why the Canter model is or is not attractive to you personally.

4. Describe three things Canter suggests doing when trying to improve the behavior of difficult-to-manage students.

Chapter 7

THE JONES MODEL
Discipline through Body Language, Incentive Systems, and
Efficient Help

CHAPTER ABSTRACT

Fredric Jones, a psychologist who develops and directs training programs in behavior management, has focused his efforts on finding remedies for the massive time wasting that, because of discipline problems, occurs in classrooms everywhere.

Jones points out that the discipline problems teachers fear most are student hostility and willful disobedience, but his studies show that problems of that nature occur less than one percent of the time. Teachers' main discipline problems, he contends, are not of the fearfully serious type but rather consist of an enormous quantity of minor transgressions, mostly of talking (80% of all discipline problems) and moving about the room without permission (over 19% of all discipline problems).

It is those two misbehaviors--unauthorized talking and movement--that are most detrimental to teacher effectiveness and student learning. They are detrimental because teachers, in dealing with them, lose great amounts of instructional time, up to 50% in typical classes.

In order to help teachers reclaim their lost teaching time, Jones devised a training program aimed at reducing to a minimum those relatively benign misbehaviors that consume so much time. His program emphasizes the acquisition of three clusters of skills--(1) using effective body language, (2) employing effective incentive systems, and (3) providing personal help efficiently.

Jones claims that good classroom discipline is maintained primarily by the first skill cluster--effective body language. Such body language includes posture, eye contact, facial expressions, signals, gestures, and physical proximity.

The second skill cluster, incentive systems, employs "Grandma's rule": "First you eat your vegetables, then you can have your dessert." In the classroom this means that students know that if (but only if) they do what they are supposed to do, they will then be given some time to do activities they most enjoy doing (the incentive).

Perhaps Jones's most surprising revelation has to do with how teachers help individual students during work time. Jones found that when teachers see students with raised hands, they usually take the student through a personal tutorial (a mini-refresher course) over what has been taught in the lesson. An astonishing average of four minutes is spent in that fashion with each student, leaving others needing help only to wait and do nothing except perhaps get into trouble. Jones trains teachers to give needed help much more efficiently, within 10 seconds up to a maximum of 20 seconds for each student. This is accomplished by using a three-step strategy: (1) quickly finding something (anything) the student has done correctly and commenting on it, (2) giving a direct hint or suggestion that will get the student started working correctly, and (3) leaving immediately.

Jones's system of discipline, then, uses body language to prevent students' goofing off, physical proximity to deal with students beginning to misbehave, incentive systems to motivate students to work and behave well, and efficient help to keep students working productively.

TERMINOLOGY

<u>Massive time wasting</u>--the large amounts of instructional time lost as teachers deal with minor misbehaviors.

<u>Body language</u>--use of the body to communicate that the teacher is calmly in control, knows what is going on, and means business; specific emphasis is given to posture, eye contact, proximity, facial expressions, and gestures.

<u>Physical proximity</u>--the teacher's positioning near a student who is beginning to misbehave.

<u>Incentive systems</u>--organized consequences (usually preferred activities) promised as rewards for good work or other behavior but delivered only after work or behavior has been accomplished.

<u>Grandma's rule</u>--"First eat your vegetables, then you can have your dessert" (the paradigm to be followed when using incentive systems).

<u>Providing efficient help</u>--giving students who need help during work time only the minimum attention required for returning them to productive work (to be accomplished in approximately 10 seconds).

APPRAISAL OF THE JONES MODEL

The Jones model, more than any other, advocates discipline techniques often used by teachers who are referred to as "naturals," meaning that they seem to do and say the right thing at the right time without having to stop and think. Like Kounin, Jones focuses on classroom efficiency, but in this case the efficiency has to do not with lessons but with personal interactions between teacher and students. The Jones model is one of the most effective available, and it has the added advantage of being easy to learn and apply with no unusual procedures.

The model is especially good at what it purports to do, which is minimize time-wasting misbehavior. That makes the model very strong in the preventive aspect of discipline. It is also powerful in supportive discipline, as it is able to redirect students who are just beginning to misbehave.

The Jones model suffers from one shortcoming, which is a lack of clear-cut steps for dealing with those rare instances of serious misbehavior that teachers fear. Jones seems to believe that such behaviors are not likely to occur when his discipline scheme is fully implemented. He does say students who are seriously misbehaving (e.g., fighting, swearing, destroying materials, and so forth) may be separated, isolated from the group, or referred to administrators, but those steps would appear to offer temporary relief, with make no provisions for long-term improvement.

• INSTRUCTORS' DISCUSSION NOTES

Use Transparency 11 to guide discussion.

Jones's Contributions to Classroom Discipline
  Explained the value of nonverbal communication in controlling behavior
  Showed how to use incentive systems to motivate good behavior
  Explained how to provide fast, efficient help to students during independent
    seatwork as a means of reducing the opportunity for misbehavior

Misbehavior--disrupts teaching and learning; causes 50% loss of teaching time.
 Of misbehavior in typical classrooms
  80% is talking without permission, such as (give examples)
  19%+ is general goofing off, such as (give examples)
  less than 1% is behavior teachers dread, such as fighting and defiance of teacher

How to Maintain Teaching Time--Use
  Body language--carriage, posture, gestures, expressions, movement
  Incentive systems, which are activities or privileges students will work for
  Efficient help, which refers to helping students who are unable to proceed on their
    own while doing individual seatwork

Body Language Skills
  Eye contact--catching the eyes of students routinely, especially those who are
    misbehaving or about to do so
  Physical proximity--moving closer or adjacent to students who are misbehaving
  or about to do so
  Body carriage--displaying self-assured posture and making movements that
    indicate composure and convey an impression of being in charge
  Facial expressions--using frowns, smiles, raised eyebrows, winks, wrinkled nose,
    grimaces, and the like, rather than words, when students seem inclined
    to misbehave
  Gestures--head shakes, nods, thumbs-up, palms up, palms down, waves,
    handshakes, open arms, and folded arms to communicate pleasure,
    displeasure, calm, acceptance, encouragement, and so forth

About Incentive Systems

Genuine incentives--use activities or privileges that all members of the class like and that can be earned by all members, not just a few.

Grandma's rule--"First eat your vegetables, then you can have dessert." (Behave as you are expected to, then you can have your reward, or incentive.)

Educational value--activities used as incentives should have educational value whenever possible: Art is a more useful incentive than talking; reading from novels is more valuable than listening to the latest popular music.

Group concern--all students must play a role in earning the incentive; misbehavior by some can harm class efforts, therefore peer pressure for good behavior is brought to bear

Ease of implementation--the incentive system must not be so complicated that it is overly burdensome for teachers; the plan must be easily workable.

How to Provide Efficient Help (during independent seatwork)

Typical concerns

Not enough time for the teacher to get to all students who request help

Students waste work time waiting for the teacher and do not complete the assignment.

Misbehavior is likely to occur when students are not working.

Students become overly dependent on the teacher's help; they don't want to work on their own.

Resolving the concerns

Arrange seating so that all students are quickly accessible to the teacher (shallow concentric circles or modular clusters)

Post graphic reminders, such as models, charts, or series of steps, that students can consult before needing to call for teacher help

Circulate quickly among students, noting their work

When help is requested, provide it in 20 seconds or less by

(1) Quickly noting anything the student has done correctly and commenting on it favorably, such as "Good work up to here."

(2) Give a clear hint or suggestion that will enable the student to proceed, such as "Invert here and multiply" or "Follow step 2 on the chart."

(3) Leave immediately (Jones says, "Be positive, be brief, and be gone.")

Jones's Reminders for Teachers

Catch misbehavior early and deal with it immediately.

Control behavior more with body language than with words.

Use physical proximity with misbehaving or defiant students.

Misbehavior

How to Maintain Teaching Time

Body Language Skills

About Incentive Systems

How to Provide Efficient Help

Jones's Reminders

SUGGESTED INSTRUCTIONAL ACTIVITIES

Assignment

1. Read assigned chapter and complete the Application Exercises as directed.

2. Make entries into notebook.

Quiz over assigned reading.

Discussion Topics

1. What is your appraisal, overall, of the Jones model of discipline?

2. If you had to choose between Jones's ideas and those of Kounin (lesson management, withitness), which would you prefer? Could they be organized into one system that would be an improvement over each individually?

3. Jones's suggestions concerning body language are said to be nothing new, that they have always been used by good teachers. Do you agree or disagree?

4. Critics of Jones's incentive systems do not like the idea of "bribing" students to work and behave well, which they are supposed to do anyway. (This same complaint is made about behavior modification.) Would you consider using incentives as he suggests? Why?

5. In classrooms where you have been, did the teacher seem to spend too much time with individual students needing help? Jones claims that many students act helpless because they want the teacher's personal attention. How would you give them the attention they want without wasting instructional time?

Small-Group Collaborative Work

1. Analyze Concept Cases 2, 3, and 4 (Sara, Joshua, and Tom) in the Application exercises. Explain how Jones would have you deal with each of those students.

2. Turn to the portion of the textbook chapter titled "A Case of Body Language in Use," where Mr. Sánchez is concerned about Sam and Jim's talking. Take turns role-playing Mr. Sánchez's part as a way of helping make effective body language second nature.

3. (a) Analyze Appendix I Scenarios 1, 7, and 8. Decide how Jones would suggest that the teacher deal with those situations.
   (b) Role-play the scenarios, taking turns playing the teacher's role.

TEST ITEMS

The following pages present true-false, multiple choice, and essay test items. Permission is granted to duplicate the items for classroom use.

Answers

True-False: 1.T, 2.F, 3.T, 4.T, 5.F, 6.F, 7.T, 8.T, 9.F, 10.T, 11.F, 12.F, 13.F, 14.T, 15.T, 16.T, 17.F, 18.T, 19.T, 20.F

Multiple Choice: 1.c, 2.b, 3.b, 4.d, 5.a, 6.c, 7.a, 8.b, 9.a, 10.c, 11.b, 12.a, 13.d, 14.c, 15.a, 16.c, 17.a, 18.d, 19.d, 20.d

Essay
1. Body language--the teacher's physical mannerisms, including eye contact, physical proximity, body carriage, facial expressions, and gestures.

Incentive systems--the organization and use of promises of rewards for desired behavior and work. The incentive (activity, tangible objects, and so forth) are given only after, and if, the desired behavior or work is shown.

Efficient help--techniques for quickly giving individual students all the help needed to keep them working productively. Jones wants teachers to aim at 10-second interventions, with a maximum of 20 seconds. The intervention consists of (1) finding anything the student has done correctly and commenting favorably on it, (2) giving a hint or direct suggestion that will get the student working again, and (3) moving away immediately.

2. (a) If excess talking is infrequent, body language would be used--eye contact, gestures, physical proximity. If talking is chronic, an incentive system would be used, in which students could earn preferred activity time if they did not talk unnecessarily for specified amounts of time.

(b) For failure to complete work during class time, the first step would be to use body language of eye contact and physical proximity, perhaps combined with individual help given quickly. If that does not work, or if the behavior is typical of many students in the class, an incentive system would be set up through which students could earn, by completing their work, a preferred activity at a later time.

(c) For students' making smart-aleck remarks, the same steps would be implemented: first, body language would be used to show clear disapproval of the remark making, and if that does not work a suitable incentive system should be implemented.

3. Jones's techniques would enhance most other models of discipline, especially as concerns body language (to show awareness, calm control, and approval/disapproval), incentive systems (for motivation and peer pressure concerning desired behavior and work output), and giving help efficiently (as a way of keeping students on task and increasing work output and quality). These three clusters of skills can easily be woven into most other models.
Credit should be given in this response for the inclusion of specific illustrative examples of Jones's techniques incorporated into another model.

Name_____ Date_____

All items refer to the JONES model. Answer each item true or false, as directed.

1. Typically, discipline problems make teachers lose approximately 50% of their instructional time.
2. Most of the lost teaching time results from students moving about the room without permission.
3. Teachers' most effective discipline technique is effective use of body language.

4. Posture is an important ingredient of good body language.

5. Eye contact, surprisingly, has been found to be relatively unimportant in maintaining discipline.
6. Eye contact is a behavior that seems to come naturally to most beginning teachers.

7. Misbehavior usually stops if the teacher makes eye contact and moves close to the offending student.
8. Learning incentives in the past have gone mainly to the best-achieving students.

9. Grandma's rule would suggest saying, "You can have five extra minutes of recess if you promise to work hard later."
10. Jones suggests using a stopwatch when implementing incentive systems.

11. Incentive systems allow good behavior to erase the penalty for previous bad behavior.

12. Jones suggests using incentive systems in ways that affect only the most poorly behaved students.
13. Teachers typically spend an average of one and one-half minutes with each student needing help.
14. Students should be seated so that the teacher can reach each of them quickly.

15. Jones doesn't want teachers to spend more than 20 seconds with each student needing help.
16. Step 3 in Jones's suggestions for providing seatwork help is "leave immediately."

17. The "dependency syndrome" refers to teachers' becoming dependent on the need to help students.
18. Jones's techniques are frequently used by teachers described as "naturals."

19. Jones would have teachers use body language rather than words in dealing with misbehavior.
20. "Incentive," as Jones uses the term, means much the same as "threat."

Name_____ Date_____

All items refer to the JONES model. Mark the single best answer, as directed.

1. Instructional time lost in most classes because of misbehavior: (a) 20%, (b) 35%, (c) 50%, (d) 65%.
2. Instructional time is best preserved through good   (a) rules, (b) body language, (c) incentives, (d) help during seatwork.
3. Most classes show a massive waste of (a) talent, (b) time, (c) resources, (d) potential.

4. The most effective body language: (a) carriage, (b) gestures, (c) facial expressions, (d) eye contact.
5. A popcorn party could serve as a/an (a) incentive, (b) proximity, (c) gesture, (d) contingency.
6. In Grandma's Rule the reward comes (a) first, (b) in the middle, (c) last, (d) incrementally.

7. The most educationally sound incentives are (a) activities, (b) money, (c) food, (d) privileges.
8. In incentive systems, use a (a) proctor, (b) stopwatch, (c) tally sheet, (d) list of demerits.

9. Student calls for teacher when help is not needed: (a) dependency syndrome, (b) unclear instructions, (c) Grandma's rule, (d) incentive breakdown.
10. Teachers should provide individual help in no more than (a) 4 minutes, (b) 1 minute, (c) 20 seconds, (d) no specific amount of time suggested.
11. During seatwork time, teachers should (a) stand at the rear of the room, (b) circulate rapidly, (c) sit beside slow students, (d) tutor individual students.
12. Misbehavior should be dealt with (a) immediately, (b) gradually, (c) intermittently, (d) slowly.
13. In discipline, body language is better than (a) gestures, (b) eye contact, (c) glares, (d) words.
14. Not part of the Jones model: (a) body posture, (b) incentives, (c) mistaken goals, (d) efficient help.
15. Incentive systems are effective because they (a) motivate, (b) punish, (c) justify, (d) ameliorate.
16. Most instructional time is lost because of excessive student (a) movement, (b) hostility, (c) talking, (d) dependency on teacher.
17. One advantage of incentive systems is that they activate (a) peer pressure, (b) body language, (c) dependency syndrome, (d) efficient help.
18. Teachers best show they mean business through their (a) voice inflection, (b) reward systems, (c) individual attention, (d) body language.
19. Fundamentally, Jones's system is most akin to that of (a) Dreikurs, (b) Ginott, (c) Redl and Wattenberg, (d) Kounin.
20. Jones's system can be implemented (a) totally, (b) partially, (c) gradually, (d) any of these.

Essay Exam: Write out your responses to the following items, as directed.

1. Name and briefly describe the three main elements (skill clusters) that make up the Jones model of discipline.

2. Indicate how the Jones model would be used to deal with the following types of misbehavior:
(a) excessive talking, (b) failure to complete assigned work during class time, and (c) students' making smart-aleck remarks.

3. Suppose you like Jones's suggestions but would like to incorporate them into another existing model of discipline. Explain how Jones's techniques could enhance the quality of the other model. For illustrative purposes, give some specific examples.

Chapter 8

THE GLASSER MODEL
Discipline through Meeting Needs without Coercion

CHAPTER ABSTRACT

William Glasser has for decades been one of the world's preeminent writers and speakers on school discipline. He is a psychiatrist, but not of the classical tradition. He believes psychiatrists waste time trying to delve into hidden causes of dysfunctional behavior. What they should do instead is help individuals clarify what they must do within the present reality in order to live successfully--hence the name for his psychiatric approach, "reality therapy."

Glasser concerns himself not just with students whose behavior is antisocial but with normal students--the typical, the average--and from an understanding of their behavior he attempts to determine how best to help all students behave properly and gain the most from school. In this approach he is, above all, pragmatic. He looks for what works without trying to fit his conclusions into any particular theoretical mold.

Glasser's beliefs about discipline have undergone significant change since first put forth in 1969. In his earlier work, presented in the acclaimed book Schools without Failure, he maintained that it was the student's responsibility to behave acceptably in school and the teacher's responsibility to help the student do so, not simply because good behavior made the classroom more pleasant but because responsible self-control was the student's ticket to personal success. Teachers, Glasser felt, were in a unique position to help because they represented for students quality adult role models, often the only such models with whom students had contact.

Within that earlier perspective, Glasser adamantly insisted that all students were in control of their own behavior, and that their behavior, good and bad, came as choices they made rationally. Good behavior led to success, while bad behavior led to failure. Teachers were to accept no excuses from students for bad behavior but were to enforce rules and continually work to help students make success-oriented decisions, a procedure that involves getting students to make value judgments about their own behavior and formulate good plans for future behavior.

By 1985, Glasser saw that the approach he had outlined and championed was not producing the results desired, in part because so many students no longer cared whether or not they did well in school. Students complained to him that school was so boring that they could muster no enthusiasm for it. Glasser likened the situation to schools' asking students to sit on a hot stove, keep still, and stop complaining about the heat.

Glasser therefore changed his position on discipline, moving the onus for good behavior away from the student and onto the school and teacher. To deal with student apathy, Glasser devised an approach that called on schools and teachers to abandon attempts to coerce students and instead to reorient schooling and teaching to meet students' basic needs.

Such needs, described in his book <u>Control Theory in the Classroom</u> (New York: Perennial Library, 1985), are five in number: survival, belonging, power, fun, and freedom. If schools are to be effective, and if teachers are to count on good behavior in the classroom, schooling must be reorganized so that those needs receive adequate attention. If that is done, school will become rewarding enough to students that most will do their work and behave responsibly.

To employ such an approach, Glasser would have teachers change their role from that of "boss-manager" (who organizes, directs, and evaluates without much input from students) to that of "lead-manager" (who realizes that genuine motivation to learn comes from within). Accordingly, teachers would devote themselves to organizing interesting learning activities and providing assistance to students. Guidance for using this approach is presented in Glasser's book <u>The Quality School: Managing Students without Coercion</u> (New York: Harper & Row, 1990). His suggestions are surprisingly nondirective, as exemplified in the following excerpt:

> Students tell me that a good teacher is deeply interested in the students and in the material being taught. They also say that such a teacher frequently conducts class discussions and does not lecture very much. Almost all of them say that a good teacher relates to them on their level; the teacher does not place herself above them, and they are comfortable talking with her. They also tell me that a good teacher does not threaten or punish and that they have little respect for teachers who do. What they are actually saying is that these are their criteria for admitting a teacher into their quality worlds.
> Students also tell me that they appreciate teachers who make an effort to be entertaining. To maintain student interest month after month in potentially boring courses, good lead-teachers try to inject humor, variety, and drama into the lessons. How to be entertaining cannot be taught: Each teacher must work it out in his or her own way, but it is another way to gain admission into students' quality worlds. (pp. 66-67)

For dealing with behavior problems, Glasser suggests an equally nondirective approach. He would have the teacher say something like "It appears we have a problem here. What can we do to work it out so we can continue with our lesson?" This approach is effective, Glasser contends, because it allows students to meet their need for power without engaging in confrontations that harm teaching, learning, and the emotions of all concerned.

TERMINOLOGY

Terminology Prior to 1985

<u>Student choice and self control</u>--students are rational beings who can control their behavior. They choose to act the way they do.

<u>Good and bad choices</u>--good choices produce good behavior. Bad choices produce bad behavior.

<u>Teachers and student choices</u>--teachers must always try to help students make good choices.

Accepting no excuses--teachers who truly care about their students accept no excuses for bad behavior.

Consequences of behavior--teachers must see to it that reasonable consequences should always follow student behavior, good or bad.

Class behavior rules--it is essential that every class have a workable list of rules to govern behavior and that those rules be consistently enforced.

Classroom meetings--classroom meetings are effective vehicles for addressing matters of class rules, behavior, and consequences. Such meetings of the entire class should be conducted regularly, with teacher and students sitting together in a closed circle, an arrangement that has come to be known as the "Glasser circle." The purpose of classroom meetings is never to find fault or assign blame but only to seek solutions to problems that concern the class.

Terminology from 1985 to Present

Motivation and behavior--all of our behavior is our best attempt to control ourselves to meet five basic needs.

The basic needs--the basic needs that students, like everyone else, continually try to satisfy are survival, belonging, power, fun, and freedom. The school experience is intimately associated with all but survival, and not infrequently with survival as well.

Needs and feelings--students feel pleasure when these needs are met, frustration when they are not.

Feelings and motivation--at least one-half of today's students will not commit themselves to learning if they find their school experience boring, frustrating, or otherwise largely dissatisfying.

Present apathy--few students in today's schools do their best work. The overwhelming majority is apathetic. Many do no schoolwork at all.

What schools must do--today's schools must create quality conditions in which fewer students and teachers are frustrated. Students must feel they belong, enjoy a certain amount of power, have some fun in learning, and experience a sense of freedom in the process.

Commitment to quality--what schools require is a new commitment to quality education, which can be accomplished through quality schools where students are encouraged, supported, and helped by the teacher.

Quality curriculum--the school curriculum should be limited to leanings that have usefulness in students' lives, and should be delivered by means of activities that attract student interest, involve students actively, provide enjoyment, and lead to meaningful accomplishments.

Quality learning--in the process of quality learning, students acquire in-depth information about topics that they recognize as being useful in their lives. They show that they have acquired such learning through demonstrating or explaining how, why, and where the leanings are of use.

Quality teaching--in quality teaching, teachers do not scold, punish, or coerce. Instead they befriend students, provide encouragement and stimulation, and show unending desire to help.

Boss managers--teachers who dictate procedures, order students to work, and berate them when they do not.

Lead managers--teachers who provide a stimulating learning environment, encourage students, and help them as much as possible.

Reality approach--directing attention to what must be done within the present situation in order to be successful.

Student needs--genetically determined requirements for survival, belonging, power, fun, and freedom.

Quality world--students' global concept of those aspects of world and life that are of value, that are worth doing and paying attention to.

Quality school (teaching, learning)-- a student evaluation in which school (or teaching or learning) is judged valuable or enjoyable enough to make participation worthwhile.

APPRAISAL OF THE GLASSER MODEL

The Glasser model, if fully implemented, might well turn out to be the most effective of all discipline systems. If student needs can be attended to as Glasser suggests, few discipline problems are likely to arise. The model would prove itself exceptionally strong in preventive discipline. Additionally, its corrective procedures would appear strong as well, assuming that misbehaving students will react as envisioned when teachers relinquish their power positions by saying, "We have a problem here. How can we work it out so that we can continue with our lesson?"

Generally speaking, teachers have always liked Glasser's suggestions. They have appreciated his common sense, nontechnical language, and sincere but low-key approach. Now they are reacting well to his new propositions concerning student needs and teacher role of lead teaching rather than boss teaching.

But concerns about Glasser's approach remain, and many questions are still to be answered. Can teaching really be reoriented as Glasser advises? Will school and curriculum permit teachers to abandon the roles of planner, director, and evaluator? Will teachers' own personalities and traditions allow them to do so? And even if teachers can make those changes, will pressures for student achievement allow teachers the luxury of spending quantities of time bringing students into lesson planning? Can so much teaching time be given over to demonstrations and lengthy discussions? Is it realistic to believe that students can or will evaluate themselves validly? And are misbehaving students likely to get back into the spirit of cooperative learning simply because the teacher asks them how the problem that is bothering them can be worked out?

These are questions, not necessarily shortcomings. As teachers are able to try out Glasser's suggestions, the questions will be answered. But that is not likely to occur immediately. Implementation of the model will take place only gradually, as teachers acquire the understandings and skills Glasser advocates.

INSTRUCTORS' DISCUSSION NOTES

Use Transparency 12 to guide discussion.

Glasser's Contributions to Classroom Discipline
    Showed how to significantly reduce behavior problems by attending to student needs
    Described quality teaching and learning, and their effects in reducing discipline
        problems
    Described how to resolve causes of student misbehavior without alienating
students
    Described how "classroom discussion circles" are used to explore and defuse potential
        causes of misbehavior as well as to resolve instances of misbehavior

School Discipline - The main problem in school discipline is not defiance or disruption; it is overwhelming student apathy toward participating in classroom activities and assignments. Students are apathetic because school does not meet their needs.

How to Help Students See School As Worthwhile
        Organize school to meet student needs
        Stress quality school work and student self-evaluation
        Abandon traditional teaching practices in favor of "quality teaching"

Student Needs that must be addressed in the classroom are those for
> Belonging--to feel oneself a genuine part of the group, class, school; to feel secure and comfortable in the classroom
>
> Power--to have some control over one's own life in school; to participate in making decisions; to have a sense of importance
>
> Fun--to do things that are enjoyable; to have access to curriculum and activities that are pleasurable rather than tedious
>
> Freedom--to be able to make choices; to be self-directing; to assume responsibility

Quality School Work and Self-Evaluation
> Within the curriculum, students help identify topics they believe will be enjoyable and useful.
>
> For topics students identify, spend the time necessary to learn them well; it is better to learn a few things very well than to cover many topics superficially.
>
> Have students explain why what they have learned is valuable to them and how the information can be used.
>
> Students are regularly asked to assess the quality of their own efforts.

Quality Teaching
Teachers provide a warm, supportive climate; they talk with students and reveal who they are and what they stand for; they review what they will and will not do on behalf of students, and they show a continual willingness to help.

Teachers ask students to do only work that is useful or that they want to learn; skills are emphasized over information; students are asked to memorize no information except that related to skills; an exception is made where information is helpful for college entrance exams.

Teachers always ask students to do the best they can; the concept of quality work is discussed regularly; work is not graded.

Teachers ask students to evaluate their work and improve it and to explain why they feel it is quality work; they are helped to use SIR--self-evaluation, improvement, and repetition until quality is achieved.

Teachers help students see that doing quality work makes them feel good; as students experience the feeling that comes with quality, they will want more of it.

Teachers help students see that quality work is never destructive to oneself, to others, or to the environment.

In these efforts, teachers function as "Lead Teachers" rather than "Boss Teachers"; they help students identify topics of possible interest, discuss with students the nature of schoolwork that might ensue, explore resources that might be useful, demonstrate possible ways of exploring the topics, emphasize quality work and student self-evaluation, and keep the classroom noncoercive and nonadversarial.

Rules and Consequences in Quality Classrooms

Students are asked to discuss class rules that will help them get their work done; these rules will ordinarily be few in number, such as "Be kind to others; Do our best work."

Teachers solicit student advice on what should be done when rules are broken; as the discussion proceeds, students will usually see that the best action is to try to remedy whatever is causing the rule to be broken; the teacher assumes responsibility for attempting to see that the problem is corrected.

Remediation is usually done by teachers' talking with offending students, assigning no blame but asking what can be done to resolve the problem so that it does not interfere with class work.

SUGGESTED INSTRUCTIONAL ACTIVITIES

Assignment

1. Read the assigned chapter.
2. Make entries into the personal notebook.

Quiz, over the assigned reading.

Discussion Topics

1. What were the major changes Glasser made in his suggestions on classroom discipline from pre-1985 to the present?

2. Overall, do Glasser's earlier or later ideas on discipline seem to make the most sense? Explain.

3. Canter's earlier approach to discipline was strongly influenced by Glasser's pre-1985 suggestions. Can you identify those major influences? (Ans: students are responsible for their behavior; they can all behave well if they want to; teachers should help students make good behavior decisions; logical consequences, positive and negative, should always follow student behavior; the teacher shows caring for students and desire to help them be successful.)

4. What is your understanding of the contrast Glasser makes between lead teachers and boss teachers? Have you seen examples of both? If so, what was your reaction to them? Is it not true that some of the most effective teachers work in the boss teacher mode (e.g., teachers in skill areas such as drama, music, athletics, and the like)? How do you explain that apparent contradiction with what Glasser says?

GLASSER ON CLASSROOM DISCIPLINE

School Discipline

How to Help Students See School as Worthwhile

Student Needs

Quality Schoolwork and Self-Evaluation

Quality Teaching

Rules and Consequences in Quality Classrooms

5. To what extent do you feel you could teach as Glasser now suggests? In which aspects would you be strong? In which would you feel uncomfortable?

6. Refer to Concept Case 4 (Tom). What would Glasser say to Tom, and how effective do you think those words would be in settling the disruption?

Small-Group Collaborative Work

1. Assign groups to discuss Concept Cases 2 and 3 and Appendix I Scenarios 1, 2, 8, 9, and 10.

2. Ask each group to select one of the designated cases or scenarios and role-play student behaviors and teacher interventions as suggested by Glasser. Share with the entire class.

TEST ITEMS

The following test items may be reproduced for classroom use.

Answers

True-False: 1.F, 2.T, 3.F, 4.T, 5.T, 6.T, 7.F, 8.T, 9.T, 10.T, 11.F, 12.T, 13.T, 14.T, 15.F, 16.F, 17.T, 18.T, 19.F, 20.T

Multiple Choice: 1.b, 2.a, 3.c, 4.d, 5.a, 6.b, 7.d, 8.a, 9.c, 10.b, 11.c, 12.c, 13.b, 14.a, 15.d, 16.d, 17.c, 18.a, 19.a, 20.c

Essay:
1. Prior to 1985 Glasser placed responsibility for behavior on students, believing all could behave properly when they so desired. Since misbehavior was a matter of choice, the teacher was to work continually in helping students make good choices that resulted in good behavior that brought success. No excuses were to be accepted. When misbehavior occurred, it was to be dealt with by having students describe their behavior, relating the behavior to class rules, and insisting that the student choose better (rule-abiding) behavior.

After 1985 Glasser placed responsibility for student behavior on school, curriculum, and teacher, maintaining that quality education could exist only in settings where students' basic needs for belonging, power, fun, and freedom were being met. This led to a changed view of the teacher's role toward one that is less demanding and coercive while also being more helpful and nonconfrontive, consistent with Glasser's depiction of lead teachers as distinct from boss teachers. When misbehavior occurs, the teacher asks students how the problem can be worked out so that the lesson can continue.

2.(a) The teacher would say quietly to Carole, "I see you are not making much progress. What can I do to help you so that you can complete your work?" Discussion continues in this vein, with teacher always asking how he or she can be more helpful.

(b) The teacher goes to Jaime and Carlos and says, "We seem to have a problem. Jaime, what is troubling you? [Listens] Carlos, what is troubling you? [Listens] How can this dispute be worked out so that both of you are satisfied and our class work can continue?"

(c) The teacher says something like "We are having a problem completing our work on time, and I think maybe it's my fault. We need to enjoy ourselves, but today we are losing too much time. How can we do this better so that we have a good time but still get our work done?"

Essay Test

Write out your answers to the following items, as directed.

1. What are the major differences between Glasser's pre-1985 model and his post-1985 model?

2. How would Glasser advise teachers to deal with the following situations:
   (a) Carole seems lazy and won't do any work.
   (b) Jaime and Carlos are having a heated argument during what is supposed to be quiet work time.
   (c) The class is having so much fun that students have begun acting outrageously silly; their work will not get completed on time.

Name_____ Date_____

All items are related to the GLASSER model. Answer each true or false, as directed.

1. Glasser now believes that individual students, not schools, bear major responsibility for behavior.
2. Before 1985, Glasser stressed that good student choices equaled good student behavior.

3. Unlike other authorities, Glasser has never advocated the use of rules for class behavior.

4. Under present conditions, no more than half our secondary students are being effectively taught.
5. Only about one out of every seven high school students is doing high-quality work.

6. The main discipline problem teachers face today is overwhelming apathy.

7. Students tell Glasser that the main problem with school is that the standards are too high.

8. Glasser claims that students' need for fun is genetically determined.

9. Students should be evaluated in terms of the quality (not the quantity) of their work.

10. Lead teachers are supposed to teach students how to self-evaluate their schoolwork.

11. "Achievement" is listed by Glasser as one of students' fundamental genetic needs.

12. Glasser says that today's curriculum lacks quality because it is too fragmented.

13. Glasser says school should be a place where students learn interesting things well.

14. Glasser says students should do written evaluations of the quality of their own work.

15. Glasser says boss teachers are the more effective at the primary level, while lead teachers are the more effective at the secondary level.
16. Glasser admits lead teachers must use coercion when recalcitrant students defy the teacher.
17. Boss teachers assume that motivation can be supplied to students from without.

18. Lead teachers make heavy use of demonstrations and good models.

19. Glasser acknowledges that many good classrooms have atmospheres that are adversarial and coercive.
20. Glasser admits that his approach to teaching will not eliminate all discipline problems.

Name_____ Date_____

All items refer to the GLASSER model. Mark the single best answer for each item, as directed.

1. Before 1985 Glasser blamed misbehavior on the (a) home, (b) student, (c) teacher, (d) school.
2. Earlier, Glasser said bad home environment was no (a) excuse, (b) obstacle, (c) disadvantage, (d) sin.
3. Earlier, Glasser said that bad behavior came from bad (a) homes, (b) attitudes, (c) choices, (d) luck.
4. Earlier, Glasser said that class rules were (a) bad, (b) futile, (c) optional, (d) essential.

5. Earlier, Glasser emphasized that teachers who care accept from their students no (a) excuses, (b) back talk, (c) flattery, (d) connivery.
6. Now Glasser says that the key to good student behavior is held by (a) parents, (b) schools, (c) administrators, (d) students.
7. Glasser now puts the onus for correcting student misbehavior on (a) home, (b) peers, (c) values, (d) schools.
8. In order to survive, schools must emphasize (a) quality, (b) standards, (c) rigor, (d) rules.

9. Students should continually judge their work's (a) value, (b) practicality, (c) quality, (d) meaning.
10. Human behavior is best understood in terms of (a) values, (b) needs, (c) customs, (d) responsibility.
11. Schools must create conditions in which teachers and students are less (a) compulsive, (b) overworked, (c) frustrated, (d) pleasure-seeking.
12. The approximate percentage of secondary students doing quality work: (a) 3, (b) 8, (c) 15, (d) 33.
13. Lead teachers stimulate students and provide (a) objectives, (b) help, (c) standards, (d) acceptance.
14. Glasser says achievement test scores are at present the accepted indicator of school (a) quality, (b) commitment, (c) choice, (d) perseverance.
15. Written evaluations of student work should be done regularly by (a) teachers, (b) outside evaluators, (c) small-group members, (d) students themselves.
16. Lead teachers are most likely to furnish (a) rules, (b) activities, (c) standards, (d) assistance.
17. When asked what should happen when rules are broken, students are likely to suggest (a) nothing, (b) forgiveness, (c) punishment, (d) extra chances.
18. Glasser would have teachers abandon (a) coercion, (b) cooperative learning, (c) rules, (d) lecturing.
19. A genetically determined need, according to Glasser: (a) fun, (b) achievement, (c) dominance, (d) cooperation.
20. Glasser wants teachers to be more (a) confrontive, (b) assertive, (c) helpful, (d) hedonistic.

Chapter 9

THE GORDON MODEL
Discipline through Developing Self-Control

CHAPTER ABSTRACT

Founder and president of Effectiveness Training International, Thomas Gordon has created an international network of instructors to provide specific kinds of training for parents, teachers, managers, young people, and others. Through his programs and books, Gordon offers strategies for teachers to help children become more self-reliant, responsible, cooperative, and self-controlled.

Gordon believes that effective discipline, both in school and in the home, cannot be achieved by means of either coercion or reward and punishment, but must instead be developed within the character of each child. He first brought his views to public attention in 1962 when he began training parents in his new program called Parent Effectiveness Training (P.E.T.). Those parents, seeing improvements in home relationships with their children, called Gordon's ideas to the attention of schools, which then began offering Teacher Effectiveness Training (T.E.T.) to their faculties. Gordon's approach placed emphasis on improving interactions between children and adults, leading to greater student responsibility.

In his 1989 book Discipline That Works, Gordon set forth for school discipline an approach that incorporated many of the principles he had earlier formulated for P.E.T. and T.E.T. He had concluded after examining school discipline policies that the punitive actions he so frequently saw were harmful to children and counterproductive in producing responsible self-control. In their place he advocated an approach in which teachers give up power authority in favor of "expertise authority," abandon reward and punishment altogether, learn to identify who "owns the problem," and apply confrontive, helping, or preventive strategies commensurate with problem ownership.

TERMINOLOGY

Authority--a condition that is used to exert influence over others

Problem--a condition, event, or situation that troubles someone

Problem ownership--the individual troubled by a condition, event, or situation, is said to "own" the problem.

Behavior window--a visual aid that helps clarify whether a problem exists and who owns it.

Active listening--involves carefully attending to and demonstrating understanding of what another person says.

Door openers--words and actions that invite others to speak about whatever is on their minds, for example, "Uh-huh. I see. Go on."

I-messages--statements in which people tell how they are being affected personally by another's behavior: "There is so much noise in here I can't talk with Adam."

You-messages--statements with a blaming tone that are leveled at other's behavior: "You have got to start paying attention."

Confrontive I-messages--messages referring to oneself that attempt to influence another to stop an unacceptable behavior: "I am very troubled by what I see."

Preventive I-messages--messages referring to oneself that attempt to forestall actions that may later constitute a problem: "I want to see how many of us remember the rules."

Preventive you-messages - accusatory messages referring to another person intended to stop that person's misbehavior. "You stop that talking now."

Shifting gears--involves changing from a confrontive posture to a listening mode, a strategy that is helpful when students resist the teacher's I-messages or defend themselves.

Participative classroom management--a leadership approach that permits students to share in problem solving and decision making regarding classroom and rules.

Communication roadblocks--types of statements well-meaning teachers say that shut down communication rather than encourage it.

Problem solving--a process in which people clarify a problem, put forth possible solutions, select a solution that is acceptable to all, implement the solution, evaluate the solution in practice, and if necessary, seek and implement yet another solution.

Traditional conflict resolution--temporarily ends disputes by producing a "winner" and a "loser," usually with detrimental effects for the loser.

No-lose conflict resolution--an approach that resolves disputes in such a way that both sides emerge as "winners."

Students' coping mechanisms--students usually deal with coercive power by fighting (against whom they have the conflict), taking flight (trying to escape the situation), or submitting (giving in to the other person).

<u>Primary feelings</u>--fundamental feelings produced by unacceptable behavior of another person (e.g., fear, disappointment).

<u>Secondary feelings</u>--feelings that are manufactured as the consequence of experiencing a primary feeling. They emerge when the difficulty is resolved; fear is replaced by anger, disappointment may be replaced by desire for revenge, and so forth.

<u>Noncontrolling methods of behavior change</u>--methods teachers can use to positively <u>influence</u> student behavior without resorting to authoritative power or rewards as a means of <u>controlling</u> student behavior.

APPRAISAL OF THE GORDON MODEL

The Gordon model has several strengths. It gives teachers a new vehicle to help students become self-reliant, make positive decisions, and control their own behavior. It moves away from the punitive/permissive extremes of discipline and identifies specific alternatives and strategies that promote self-discipline in children. In addition, Gordon provides teachers with a visual "window" to help them clarify the concept of problem ownership and subsequently take appropriate action to resolve classroom misbehavior.

But the Gordon model presents obstacles as well. One is that in order to use the model properly, teachers must give up their traditional concept of misbehavior and replace it with the belief that student behavior is <u>mis</u>behavior only when it troubles the teacher--a relativistic notion that some teachers find hard to accept. Further, many teachers with difficult-to-manage classes do not consider students to be as well-intentioned as Gordon seems to imply; those teachers will be reluctant to abandon techniques that, though controlling of students, do maintain order and allow instruction to occur. Finally, questions remain whether teachers, being neither psychologists nor trained counselors, can easily acquire skills for applying interventions even when they have determined who owns the problem.

INSTRUCTORS' DISCUSSION NOTES

Use Transparency 13 to guide discussion.

Gordon's Contributions to Classroom Discipline
       Introduced the concept of "problem ownership."
       Used the "behavior window" to illustrate problem ownership.
       Explained confrontive, helping, and preventive techniques that are useful in
              classroom discipline and showed that problem ownership indicates
              which should be used.
       Helped explain why neither reward nor punishment is effective in classroom
              discipline.
       Introduced new concepts important in classroom discipline, including:
              Students' coping mechanisms of fighting against, fleeing from, or
              submitting to, when faced with coercive power.
       Introduced the No-Lose method of conflict resolution, which helps disputants
              find solutions that are satisfactory to everyone.
       Clarified primary and secondary feelings that teachers can experience following a
              student's behavior: primary feelings are fundamental (hurt,
              disappointment); secondary feelings (anger, desire for revenge) often
              emerge after the problem is resolved. Teachers should act on their
              primary, not secondary, feelings.
       Explained roadblocks to communication, twelve in number, that tend to shut
              down communication. Examples are giving orders, preaching, and
              advising. Teachers should avoid using the roadblocks.

Discipline--The only truly effective discipline is <u>self-control</u>, developed internally in each
       student. To develop student self-control, teachers must give up their power
       (controlling) authority and replace it with influence or persuasive authority.

Misbehavior and Who Owns the Problem
       "Misbehavior" is a specific action of a child that produces an undesirable consequence
              for an adult. It is a concept held by adults, not by children.
       Whoever is bothered by a behavior is said to "own" the problem. Teachers bothered by
              student behavior own the problem and are motivated to do something about it.
       In the classroom, the strategies employed to resolve behavior difficulties depend on
              who owns the problem, the teacher or the student.
       The "behavior window" is a graphic device used to illustrate who owns the problem
              and what can best be done to resolve it.

THE BEHAVIOR WINDOW

Student's behavior is causing a problem for the student only. STUDENT OWNS THE PROBLEM
Student's behavior is not causing a problem for either student or teacher. NO PROBLEM EXISTS (this is the no-problem area of the behavior window)
Student's behavior is causing a problem for the teacher. TEACHER OWNS THE PROBLEM

Discipline Skills that Teachers Apply in Accordance with Problem Ownership
  When the TEACHER owns the problem, use Confrontive Skills
  When there is NO PROBLEM to own, use Preventive Skills
  When the STUDENT owns the problem, use Helping Skills

BEHAVIOR WINDOW	TEACHER SKILLS
Student's behavior is causing a problem for the student only. STUDENT OWNS THE PROBLEM	HELPING SKILLS
Student's behavior is not causing a problem for either the student or the teacher. NO PROBLEM EXISTS	PREVENTIVE SKILLS
Student's behavior is causing a problem for the teacher. TEACHER OWNS THE PROBLEM	CONFRONTIVE SKILLS

Confrontive, Helping, and Preventive Skills
> Confrontive Skills (when the teacher owns the problem)
>> Modify the environment through enrichment or limiting distractors
>> Identify and respond to teacher's own primary feeling of disappointment, fear, or worry that may be bringing anger to the situation
>> Send I-messages instead of you-messages
>> Shift gears by attentive listening when students become defensive
>> Use the no-lose method of conflict resolution
> Helping Skills (when the student owns the problem)
>> Use listening skills - passive listening, acknowledgment, door openers, and active listening
>> Avoid communication roadblocks such as giving orders, preaching, and so forth
> Preventive Skills (when no problem exists)
>> Use preventive I-messages, e.g., "I'd like us all to pay close attention on this problem."
>> Set rules of classroom behavior collaboratively
>> Use participative management in solving problems and making decisions

Why Reward and Punishment Does Not Work
> Teachers use rewards believing they will help students behave responsibly, but
> Rewards are counterproductive because
>> Students become concerned only with the reward, not with good behavior
>> When rewards are removed, students revert to improper behavior
>> When students accustomed to rewards do not receive them, they feel they are being punished
> Punishment is equally ineffective because
>> It makes students feel belittled, hostile, and angry
>> It decreases student desire to cooperate
>> Students lie and cheat to avoid punishment
>> It teaches that might makes right

THOMAS GORDON ON DISCIPLINE

> Discipline

> Misbehavior and Who Owns the Problem

THE BEHAVIOR WINDOW

Discipline Skills and the Behavior Window

BEHAVIOR WINDOW   TEACHER SKILLS

Confrontive, Helping, and Preventive Skills

Why Rewards and Punishment Do Not Work

SUGGESTED INSTRUCTIONAL ACTIVITIES

Assignment

1. Read chapter and make entries into notebook.
2. Complete application exercises as directed.

Quiz over the assigned reading.

Discussion Topics

1. In what ways are the ideas of Glasser and Gordon similar? How are they different?

2. The behavior window that Gordon uses to help individuals visualize problem ownership is not a static window. Rather, the areas can move, depending on the teacher's mood, the situation, and the student. Does this flexibility encourage preferential treatment for nontroublemakers and unfair treatment for students with more severe problems?

3. Some educators, concerned that school not be thought of as a factory, are against the Gordon model. In what ways is the factory model an accurate description of schooling? Is the factory model appropriate for today's schooling and needs?

Small-Group Collaborative Work

1. In groups of four or five, analyze Concept Cases 2, 3, and 4 at the end of the chapter. Indicate how Gordon would have you deal with the situations depicted. Present your conclusions for class discussion.

2. Review the Scenarios in Appendix I. Select two of them and indicate how the Gordon model would be applied to those situations. Present your conclusions for discussion.

TEST ITEMS

The following pages provide test items related to the Gordon model. Permission is granted to duplicate the items for classroom use.

Answers

True-False: 1.T, 2.F, 3.F, 4.F, 5.F, 6.F, 7.T, 8.T, 9.F, 10.F, 11.T, 12.F, 13.T, 14.T, 15.F, 16.F, 17.F, 18.F, 19.T, 20.T

Multiple Choice: 1.b, 2.d, 3.d, 4.b, 5.c, 6.a, 7.a, 8.b, 9.c, 10.b, 11.a, 12.d, 13.b, 14.b, 15.b, 16.a, 17.d, 18.b, 19.c, 20.a

Essay:
1. If yes: school is the workplace for students to complete projects and products that show their learning (product focus). If no: school is a place for students to learn socialization and life skills (humanistic focus).
2. Strengths: Teachers visualize problem ownership in order to clarify problems and identify appropriate action, and they have specific alternatives and strategies, including participative management and no-lose conflict resolution, to better help students become self-reliant, make positive decisions, and control their own behavior. Limits: Most teachers are not trained as counselors or psychologists to easily acquire and use the skills. Also, teachers may have difficulty changing their perception of student misbehavior and problem ownership.

3. May include: no-lose conflict resolution, participative management, problem solving, and effective communication strategies such as active listening and I-messages.

4. Both utilize participative management and effective problem-solving strategies. Gordon identifies different types of authority and redefines misbehavior; he visualizes problem ownership with a behavior window; and he advocates a no-lose method of conflict resolution. Glasser believes that everyone has basic needs and that schools and teaching must be reoriented to meet students' basic needs. Glasser also describes quality schools, quality teachers, and a quality world where the concepts students hold of the world and life are of value, worth doing and worth paying attention to. To forward quality, teachers must function as lead-managers (not boss-managers) who provide for and encourage quality experiences for their students, and who teach students how to evaluate themselves.

Name _____ Date _____

All items on this page relate to the GORDON model. Answer true or false as directed.

1. The Gordon model of behavior management evolved from his earlier work with parent and teacher effectiveness training.
2. One strategy Gordon advocates is rewarding students with tokens and certificates for good behavior.
3. Gordon's examination of school discipline policies confirms that punishment is, after all, the best way to control student behavior.
4. Authority is essentially a fairly simple concept with a relatively clear meaning in the classroom.
5. The behavior window is a visual aid for use in analyzing the severity of misbehavior.

6. I-messages are intended to remind students that the teacher is in charge of the situation.

7. Door openers are invitations for an individual to talk more, go deeper, or even to begin to talk, about a concern.
8. When teachers shift gears they change from a sending-assertive posture to one of listening and trying to understand.
9. Communication roadblocks are techniques teachers use to reduce the amount of student talk.
10. Participative management is appropriate in the Japanese workplace but not in American schools.
11. Passive listening is an effective technique for teachers to use when students want to discuss problems.
12. Gordon advocates a no-lose conflict resolution process in which disputants share control and the teacher proposes the solution.
13. Students may cope with coercive problems by fighting, running away from the problem, or withdrawing.
14. Primary feelings are the initial emotions teachers usually experience when students behave unacceptably.
15. Authority E is earned because of the position a person holds with a company or group.

16. Authority C, because it comes from individuals who care, is a positive way to influence others.
17. Students respond well and make positive changes in behavior when given rewards.

18. Gordon believes adults and children have a common, mutual understanding of what is meant by "misbehavor."
19. Teachers can influence student behavior by modifying the classroom environment.

20. When teachers use preventive I-messages, they try to influence the student to act a certain way in the future.

Name _____ Date _____

All items on this page relate to the GORDON model. Select the single best answer, as directed.

1. "Today, class, Mr. Tenfeathers, a jeweler, will tell us about Navajo jewelry making." This exemplifies (a) Authority E, (b) Authority J, (c) Authority C, or (d) Authority P.
2. "If you can't work quietly, you'll have to finish this at home." This is an example of (a) Authority E, (b) Authority J, (c) Authority C, (d) Authority P.
3. The least effective form of authority for influencing positive behavior change is (a) Authority E, (b) Authority J, (c) Authority C, (d) Authority P.
4. When a student is frustrated because he or she doesn't understand the lesson, the problem belongs to (a) the class, (b) the student, (c) the teacher, (d) the student's parents.
5. When a student annoys the teacher by asking irrelevant questions, the problem for certain belongs to (a) everyone, (b) the student, (c) the teacher, (d) the student's parents.
6. The behavior window is (a) a visualization tool that changes, (b) a fixed visualization tool for problem ownership, (c) used to assess teacher behavior, (d) a behavior hierarchy.
7. Rewards see, effective because (a) they produce immediate results, (b) teachers remain in charge, (c) their influence is long-lasting, (d) they facilitate learning.
8. Which category of coping mechanisms best describes the behavior of a student who drops out of school? (a) fight, (b) flight, (c) mediation, (d) submission.
9. Successful conflict resolution (a) leaves the teacher in control, (b) gives power to the student, (c) results in a no-lose situation, (d) results from outside arbitration.
10. Which of the following would best help students stay focused on learning? (a) walls in primary colors, (b) theme centers, (c) popular music, (d) desks arranged in rows.
11. "If you had made a list of the steps like I said, you could have done your work easily!" This is most likely (a) advising, (b) lecturing, (c) preaching, (d) warning.
12. "If you don't first make a list of the steps you need to do for this activity, you are likely to make a mistake that will throw you off." This is (a) advising, (b) lecturing, (c) preaching, (d) warning.
13. "You girls must stop making so much noise." This is an example of (a) I-message, (b) confrontive you-message, (c) shifting gears, (d) problem ownership.
14. Student involvement is encouraged in (a) authoritarianism, (b) participative management, (c) the problem window, (d) I-messages.
15. Reward is an example of (a) influence technique, (b) controlling technique, (c) collaborative technique, (d) coping technique.
16. An example of a typical primary feeling: (a) fear, (b) attack, (c) revenge, (d) avoidance.

17. The appropriate skills cluster when the student owns the problem: (a) confrontive, (b) preventive, (c) corrective, (d) helping.
18. Good I-messages are most often (a) preventive, (b) confrontive, (c) helping, (d) resolving.

19. Listening is a skill of (a) prevention, (c) confrontation, (c) helpfulness, (d) correction.

20. In passive listening, the teacher (a) says nothing, (b) makes reflective comments, (c) makes clarifying comments, (d) summarizes the student's comments.

Essay Exam. Write out your answers to the following items, as directed.

1. The Gordon model contains elements similar to Deming's teachings in the Japanese workplace. Is school an appropriate environment for this type of model? Why/why not?

2. Describe what generally are considered to be the strengths and limitations of the Gordon model. Explain why this model is or is not attractive to you personally.

3. Looking to the needs of the future, what life skills stressed by Gordon will be needed by students for them to be successful in a global society?

4. Contrast the Gordon model with Glasser's emphasis on quality in managing behavior.

Chapter 10

THE CURWIN AND MENDLER MODEL
Discipline through Dignity and Hope

CHAPTER ABSTRACT

Richard Curwin and Allen Mendler have made major contributions to school discipline in the form of strategies for improving classroom behavior through maximizing student dignity and hope. They set forth their views in two main publications--Discipline with Dignity, which they coauthored in 1988, and Rediscovering Hope: Our Greatest Teaching Strategy, authored by Curwin in 1992.

Their ideas have been especially useful to teachers who work with chronically misbehaving students. Those students--about 5% of the student population, Curwin and Mendler say--typically disrupt instruction, interfere with learning, and make life miserable for teachers. Described as "without hope," such students are doomed to fail unless treated with special consideration and care. Curwin and Mendler explain what without-hope students need if they are to have a chance for success in school, and they provide strategies to help teachers reclaim those students.

If they are to rescue without-hope students, teachers must accept and apply five major principles regarding interactions with students. They are:

> *Dealing with misbehavior is an important part of teaching.
> *Lasting results are only achieved over time.
> *Student dignity must be preserved.
> *Good discipline must not interfere with student motivation.
> *Responsibility is more important than obedience.

TERMINOLOGY

Behaviorally at risk--students whose chronic classroom misbehavior puts them in imminent danger of failing in school

Dignity--value placed on human life. Students do all they can to prevent damage to their dignity, or their own sense of worth.

<u>Hope</u>--most chronically misbehaving students have lost all hope of encountering anything worthwhile in school and of having some measure of control over their lives.

<u>School's professionals and clients</u>--schools exist for students, not teachers. Teachers' role is to do all they can to help students learn and behave responsibly.

<u>Five underlying principles of effective discipline</u>--discipline is a very important part of teaching. Short-term solutions are rarely effective. Students must always be treated with dignity. Discipline must not interfere with motivation to learn. Responsibility is more important than obedience.

<u>Short-term solutions</u>--quick solutions such as writing names on the board are often long-term disasters because they damage student dignity, which reduces motivation, increases resistance, and promotes desire for revenge.

<u>Responsibility versus obedience</u>--responsibility involves making enlightened decisions and almost always produces better long-term behavior changes than does obedience to teacher demands.

<u>Dimensions of discipline</u>--a thorough discipline approach includes prevention (steps taken to forestall misbehavior), action (steps taken when class rules are broken), and resolution (special arrangements for improving the misbehavior of out-of-control students).

<u>Consequences</u>--preplanned actions invoked when class rules are broken. Consequences are planned by the teacher with student input and agreement.

<u>The social contract</u>--a written agreement concerning class rules and consequences, signed by teacher and students.

<u>Insubordination rule</u>--a bottom-line rule included in the social contract stating that whenever a student refuses to accept the consequence for breaking a rule, that student will not be allowed back into the class until he or she accepts the consequence. This rule requires support of the school administrator.

<u>Creative responses</u>--unexpected responses to misbehavior that teachers can at times use effectively.

<u>Preventing escalation</u>--to avoid typical confrontations in which teacher and student both try to "win" the argument, wise teachers use active listening, I-messages, and private discussion to de-escalate these situations.

<u>Motivating the difficult-to-manage student</u>--teachers can motivate students or improve their behavior by providing interesting lessons on topics of personal relevance that permit active involvement and lead to competencies students value.

APPRAISAL OF THE CURWIN AND MENDLER MODEL

The Curwin and Mendler model has several strengths. It is based on the primary tenets that student dignity must be preserved and that lasting results are only achieved over time. It offers teachers realistic help for understanding and working with students who chronically misbehave. The social contract and the insubordination rule are concrete tools for teachers to use with behaviorally at-risk students.

A major obstacle teachers encounter in adopting the model is the changes they must make concerning their roles and responsibilities. They must recognize that schools exist for students, not teachers; that teachers are professionals whose reason for existence is to benefit students, who are their clients; that the teachers' role is simple--to do everything possible to help students learn and behave responsibly. In this role, teachers must calmly accept being called nasty names, acknowledge that slanderous expletives leveled at them may be partially correct, and all the while keep wanting and trying to help the very students who spurn their efforts. They must also accept that change will occur slowly, if at all, but sincerely believe that the students are worth every effort.

INSTRUCTORS' DISCUSSION NOTES

Use Transparency 14 to guide discussion.

Curwin and Mendler's Contributions to Discipline
    Pointed out the importance of maintaining students' sense of dignity
    Showed that restoring hope is essential for students who are at risk of failing for
        reasons of behavior--students referred to as lazy, losers, with bad attitudes
    Provided strategies for teachers to help the "lost students" who are behaviorally at risk
    Emphasized that teachers, the professionals, should do all in their power to help
        students, their clients, behave responsibly

Discipline--Effective discipline must emphasize responsibility more than obedience, treat
    students with dignity, and never interfere with motivation to learn. This is true for all
    students, and especially for those referred to as "behaviorally at risk."

Students Who Are Behaviorally At Risk (of failing because of misbehavior)
    Are making poor or failing grades
    Have received, but do not respond to, ordinary punishments and consequences, such as
        praise, scoldings, rewards, and staying in after school
    Have low self-concepts in relation to school, as shown in apathy and reluctance to try
    Have little or no hope of finding success in school
    Associate with other "hopeless" students who mutually reinforce each other

Principles of Discipline for the Behaviorally At Risk
  Put as much effort into teaching good behavior as into teaching content
  Do not rely on short-term solutions, such as writing students' names on the board,
       scolding, keeping students in after class, or using sarcasm. These
       damage student self-image and provoke additional disobedience.
  Always treat each student with dignity, which means showing concern for needs,
       trying to understand viewpoints, and treating the student as you yourself
       would like to be treated.
  Make sure that any discipline technique used does not damage students'   motiva
                                                                           tion to
                                                                           learn.
  Provide opportunities for students to exercise responsibility through continually
       offering them choices rather than giving them commands they are to
       obey.
  Always look for ways to help the student.

Contents of an Effective Discipline Plan
  The Prevention Dimension
       With student collaboration, develop clear, brief rules of classroom behavior.
       Establish a list of consequences to be invoked when rules are broken.
       Write up the plan of rules and consequences; ask students to agree to them and
       sign as a "social contract."
       Treat students as individuals; this means they often will not be treated equally.
  The Action Dimension
       When rules are broken, look upon the situation as an opportunity to interact
            productively with the student.
       Invoke consequences, but avoid power struggles
       Remain positive and mindful of student dignity
  The Resolution Dimension
       Try to find out what will prevent the problem's occurring again, and
       With the student, make a plan for future positive action
       Implement and monitor the plan; modify it if necessary

When Consequences Must Be Invoked
>Always invoke a consequence when a rule is broken.
>Take into account the offense, situation, student involved, and best means of helping that particular student.
>To the offending student, state the rule and consequence. Nothing more need be said.
>Do not embarrass the student; keep the situation private if possible; do not get involved in a power struggle.
>Control your anger by keeping calm and speaking quietly, but accept no excuses.
>When possible, let the student select the consequence from a list of alternatives.
>When normal consequences do not work, try creative responses such as reversing roles with the student or making an audio- or videotape of the class.
>If the situation threatens to escalate, use active listening and arrange to speak with the student at a later time.

Motivate the Difficult to Motivate by
>Maximizing personal importance and relevance for the students.
>Involving students actively in lessons--use senses, talk, move about; make lessons fun.
>Show your own genuine energy and interest in the topic; each day do at least one activity that you love.
>Make class something students look forward to; make them wonder what will happen next.

CURWIN AND MENDLER ON DISCIPLINE

Discipline

Students Who Are Behaviorally At Risk

Principles of Discipline for the Behaviorally At Risk

Contents of an Effective Discipline Plan

When Consequences Must Be Invoked

Motivating the Difficult to Motivate

SUGGESTED INSTRUCTIONAL ACTIVITIES

Assignment

1. Read the chapter and make entries into notebook.
2. Complete application exercises as directed.

Quiz over the assigned reading.

Discussion Topics

1. How do you think the Curwin and Mendler model compares with others you have learned about for handling chronically misbehaving students? Be explicit.

2. Curwin says these at-risk students are disruptive and difficult because their dignity and hope have been taken away. How can teachers help students if this is the students' own perception of their lives?

3. "At risk" is a term that has been used and misused by many to describe the segment of the student population who are in danger of failing for various reasons. How is Curwin and Mendler's use of the term different from this common understanding?

4. Curwin and Mendler propose that schools exist for students, not for teachers, and that as professionals teachers must be willing to tolerate disgusting student behavior as they try to help students learn and behave responsibly. Why do you agree or disagree with this viewpoint?

5. How effective do you think social contracts and insubordination rules will be for students who do not want to be in the classroom and who find suspension an attractive alternative?

Small Group Collaborative Work

1. In groups of four or five, analyze Concept Cases 2, 3, and 4 at the end of the chapter. Indicate how Curwin and Mendler would have you deal with the situations depicted. Present your conclusions for class discussion.

2. Select two of the Scenarios in Appendix I. Indicate how the Curwin and Mendler model would be applied to those situations. Present your conclusions to the class for discussion.

TEST ITEMS

The following pages provide test items related to the Curwin and Mendler model. Permission is granted to duplicate the items for classroom use. Answers are given here:

True-False: 1.F, 2.F, 3.T, 4.F, 5.T, 6.F, 7.F, 8.T, 9.T, 10.T, 11.F, 12.F, 13.F, 14.T, 15.T, 16.F, 17.T, 18.T, 19.F, 20.F

Essay:
1. If yes: Teachers' role is to do all they can to help students learn and behave responsibly. If no: Teachers are professionals who should be respected and supported because of their knowledge and training. Open to alternatives.

2. Strengths: Basic tenets support the model: student dignity, motivation, responsibility, and progress over time are essential for lasting results. The social contract and the insubordination rule are concrete teacher tools.

Limitations: Teachers may find it hard to behave in accordance with the principles that school exists solely for students' benefit, that teachers must be accepting of bad treatment students give them and the class, and that they are obliged to continue trying to help students who disdain their efforts.

3. According to Curwin and Mendler, "at risk" refers to what students do under the conditions they are in, not who they are. These students have stopped learning, no longer make an effort, have stopped believing that school can make a positive difference in their lives, and often behave hurtfully toward teachers and other students.

4. Curwin and Mendler stress the following to teachers of at-risk students:

> Dealing with misbehavior is a very important part of teaching.
> Lasting changes in behavior are only achieved over time.
> Student dignity must be preserved.
> Good discipline must not interfere with student motivation.
> Responsibility is more important than obedience.

5. Curwin and Mendler: In light of their understandings of at-risk and dignity, Curwin and Mendler propose five principles regarding teacher interaction with at-risk students; they redefine school's existence and teachers' roles; and they present a thorough discipline approach of prevention, action, and resolution, with a social contract, consequences, and an insubordination rule. Further, they describe several creative teacher responses to misbehavior.

Canter: Teachers have the right to teach without disruption and students have the right to learn in a safe, supportive atmosphere. When students misbehave it is because they are ignorant of what is expected or else they simply enjoy misbehaving. Assertive teachers clearly and firmly communicate wants, needs, and limits and are prepared to back up words with appropriate actions. They also teach students exactly how they are expected to behave in various classroom situations.

Name _____ Date _____

All items relate to the CURWIN AND MENDLER model. Write T or F to the left of each item.

1. Curwin and Mendler define "at-risk" students as loners who avoid other problem students.

2. Short-term solutions to discipline problems can usually evolve into good long-term solutions.
3. Students do all in their power to prevent damage to their self-image.

4. Students who break rules will be allowed to return to the classroom after they apologize for their inappropriate behavior.
5. Teachers need to recognize that sometimes hostile students are partially correct in their accusations and name-calling.
6. About 25% of the total student population can be considered out-of-control.

7. At-risk students will be motivated to learn if they perceive the topic to be attractive, even if they are unsuccessful in their effort.
8. Scolding, lecturing, extra work, isolation, and trips to the principal's office have little effect on students who chronically misbehave.
9. Teachers and students should share in formulating class rules and consequences.

10. For best results, every rule should have a list of possible consequences established in advance.
11. Extra written assignments, extra math problems, and running extra laps are examples of instructional consequences.
12. Creative responses to chronic misbehavior usually make problem situations worse.

13. By switching roles, the teacher and student are made to experience increased frustration about the problem situation.
14. In the long run, a student's responsibility and ability to make good decisions are more valuable goals than obeying the teacher's wishes.
15. It is important that discipline techniques not interfere with students' motivation to learn.

16. Weekly teacher temper tantrums help build better behavior in students.

17. Teachers must put as much effort into teaching behavior as they put into teaching content.

18. Because students have different needs, it is all right to treat them differently when they are being disciplined.
19. Teachers may lose face or appear less in control and will consequently become less effective in controlling the class if they accept put-downs from students.
20. A social contract keeps students and teachers aware of favored events and activities for the year.

Name _____ Date _____

Items relate to the Curwin and Mendler Model. Write the letter of the best answer to the left of each item.

1. Dignity is most closely related to (a) articulation, (b) peer standing, (c) poise, (d) self-image.
2. Schools exist solely for the benefit of (a) administrators, (c) counselors, (c) students, (d) teachers.
3. Of the total student population, (a) 5%, (b) 10%, (c) 15%, or (d) 25% are described as "at risk" of failing because of behavior problems.
4. Greg teaches the class while Mr. Santos sits at Greg's desk and reenacts Greg's behavior. This technique is called (a) creativity, (b) improbability, (c) paradox, (d) role reversal.
5. Ms. Costa says, "Wow, Julia! Don't do your homework again tonight and you'll hold a new record for missed assignments. Tomorrow we can celebrate!" This is an example of (a) creative response, (b) humor, (c) paradoxical behavior, (d) role reversal.
6. Adam calls Mr. Bennett blind when the teacher asks him to stop tapping his pencil; Mr. Bennett responds, "That's possible. I haven't had my eyes checked lately." This response is termed (a) creative (b) improbable (c) paradoxical (d) put-down.
7. Students should be corrected (a) in front of the student's friends, (b) in front of another teacher for that teacher's support, (c) in front of the entire class, (d) in private.
8. Time out and suspension are examples of which type of consequence? (a) conventional, (b) generic, (c) instructional, (d) logical.
9. (a) Conventional consequences, (b) generic consequences, (c) instructional consequences, (d) logical consequences require students to make right what they have done wrong.
10. Reminders and warnings that are invoked for almost all misbehavior are examples of which type of consequence? (a) conventional, (b) generic, (c) instructional, (d) logical.
11. Students are most likely to be motivated in lessons that are (a) excessively challenging, (b) passively engaging, (c) personally relevant, (d) repetitive.
12. The social contract (a) reminds administrators of PTA events, (b) reminds students and teachers of class rules and consequences, (c) reminds students of scheduled activities, (d) reminds teachers of school events.
13. The (a) action dimension, (b) insubordination rule, (c) logical consequences, (d) resolution dimension excludes a student from class until he or she accepts the consequence.
14. Curwin and Mendler apply the term "at risk" to students who have (a) alcohol or drug addictions, (b) serious behavior problems, (c) low self-value, (d) unstable homes.
15. The number of behaviorally at-risk students is (a) declining steadily, (b) increasing steadily, (c) holding steady.
16. Writing names on the board is an example of (a) a long-term solution, (b) a no-lose resolution, (c) a short-term solution, (d) an action disclaimer.
17. Consequences administered for misbehavior should be (a) preplanned, (b) spontaneous, (c) natural, (d) embarrassing to the student.
18. The Curwin and Mendler model is especially good for (a) halting misbehavior, (b) forming bonds with parents, (c) speeding learning, (d) improving chronic misbehavior.
19. Teachers (a) are the most important members of the class, (b) are there to serve students, (c) should accept no nonsense from students, (d) have secondary status in the class.
20. The social contract is (a) an oral agreement, (b) drawn up legally, (c) written out, (d) enforceable before the school board.

<u>Essay Exam</u>. Write out your answers to the following items, as directed.

1. Curwin and Mendler believe teachers must calmly accept being called nasty names and other verbal abuse as they try to help at-risk students in their class. Is this a reasonable expectation of a professional? Would another alternative be better? Explain your views.

2. Describe what generally are considered to be the strengths and limitations of the Curwin and Mendler model. Explain why this model is or is not attractive to you personally.

3. Without stereotyping, describe the behavior of students Curwin and Mendler call "at risk."

4. What are the five principal reminders that Curwin and Mendler give teachers who work with behaviorally at-risk students?

5. Contrast the Curwin and Mendler model with Canter's Assertive Discipline approach to correcting misbehavior.

Chapter 11

CLASSROOMS THAT ENCOURAGE GOOD BEHAVIOR

CHAPTER ABSTRACT

Student behavior is affected significantly by three components of classroom organization--(1) the person component, (2) the management component, and (3) the teacher component. All three can contribute strongly to good preventive discipline.

The person component focuses on students' self-concept and self-respect, in the belief that students who respect themselves (and consequently others) behave better in the classroom. This component emphasizes (1) regular personal attention from the teacher (acknowledgment, support, encouragement, urging, and trust), (2) frequent genuine success in learning (involving realistic goals, a curriculum for competence, good directions and help, effective instructional materials, and esprit de corps), and (3) recognition for accomplishments (charting personal and group gains, informing parents, sharing in the classroom, and producing class newsletters).

The management component focuses on how teachers organize, deliver, monitor, and communicate their programs. Good management encourages good behavior by eliminating confusion and "dead spots" in lessons. In addition it motivates students through an atmosphere of support and helpfulness.

Management has much to do with the atmosphere, usually called "classroom climate," that refers to the feeling tone in the classroom. Poor climates are characterized as cold, demanding, unfriendly, and threatening, while good climates are warm, friendly, supportive, and pleasant. Establishing a good climate requires attention to human relations skills (friendliness, positive attitude, ability to listen, ability to compliment genuinely, willingness to help, and modeling desired behavior).

Management also focuses on improving relationships with parents, which brings highly desirable support and encouragement from home. Parental support is obtained through communication (notes, phone calls, newsletters, and personal conferences) that shows respect for parents and interest in their children. Such communication should be clear and concise, without educational jargon. It should describe the educational program, expectations of students, and roles parents can play. It should not give advice to parents on how to raise their children, nor should it criticize students, a sore point for parents, but rather should indicate areas of learning and personal growth that are to receive attention.

Finally, good management ensures a smooth-running classroom, where routines are in place that maximize productive work while minimizing disruptions. Routines are especially helpful during (1) opening and closing activities (kept quick, clean, and productive); (2) distribution, use, and collection of materials (often accomplished with several student assistants); (3) disposition of completed work (placement, collection, storage); and (4) assistance given to students at work (clear understanding of expectations, models to emulate, quick and efficient monitoring, and proper help).

The teacher component focuses on various teacher traits and the effect those traits have on students. Certain traits seem to encourage cooperation and productive work while others seem to provoke disruption and disobedience.

Teachers most effective in promoting good classroom behavior seem to anticipate problems and take steps to prevent them. Their personalities are attractive to students (relaxed, attentive, interesting, humorous). At the same time, good teachers are serious about learning and teaching (efficient, organized, show good planning) and equally serious about feelings, as shown through their behavior toward students (warm, flexible, interesting, and hard-working, with standards that they try hard to help students attain).

INSTRUCTORS' DISCUSSION NOTES

Use Transparency 15 to guide discussion.

Classroom Components that Encourage Good Behavior
> Goal: To establish classrooms that are warm, nurturing, helpful, and accepting, while at the same time efficiently run with high levels of achievement. These traits combine to curtail student misbehavior. Teachers can work toward such classrooms by giving attention to three components of effective classrooms--the person component, the management component, and the teacher component.

The Person Component--In this component attention is given to the following:
> Strengthening student self-Concept
>> Giving each student personal attention daily, by . . .
>> Ensuring student success academically and socially, by . . .
>> Building esprit de corps by
>>> Instilling a sense of togetherness through group enterprises, such as . . .
>>> Building sense of purpose into class activities--personal or group gains
>>> Arranging for public recognition for class accomplishments, by . . .
>>> Informing and involving parents.

The Management Component--1. Classroom Climate
Climate refers to the "feeling tone" of the classroom.
Desirable climates are warm, friendly, supportive, helpful, and interesting.
Undesirable climates are cold, threatening, demanding, and demeaning.
Classroom climate depends primarily on how teachers manage human relations with
    attention to
        General human relations skills
            Showing friendliness by . . .
            Maintaining a positive attitude, shown when one . . .
            Listening attentively to others
            Learning to give and receive genuine compliments
        Additional human relations skills used with students
            Giving regular personal attention
            Showing continual willingness to help
            Modeling courtesy and good manners
        Additional human relations skills used with parents
            Maintaining regular communication by . . .
            Clearly describing program, expectations, evaluation, and home
                responsibilities
            Never criticizing child to parents; speaking instead of plans for helping
                child
            Learning to conference productively with parents by . . .
            Being judicious in giving advice to parents--do's and don'ts such as . . .

The Management Component--2. Classroom Routines
Class routines clarify the procedures of day-to-day activities, such as
        How one opens and closes activities to reduce misbehavior
            Open activities by getting immediate attention or getting immediately to
                work.
            Close activities by summarizing and cleaning up or returning materials.
        How one makes use of instructional materials
            Obtain or distribute materials quickly by . . .
            When finished, collect or replace materials quickly by . . .
            Establish an efficient routine for completed work, such as . . .
        How one makes use of student assistants (for help and for student sense of
            classroom ownership)
            Provide helpful jobs for everyone, if possible, such as . . .
        How one helps students doing individual work
            Make sure they know exactly what to do and how to do it.
            Provide a written or graphic model for guidance.
            Circulate among students to observe, encourage, and help.
            Give help succinctly. (Recall Fredric Jones's suggestions.)

The Teacher Component--This component focuses on teacher traits that affect discipline.
Three general types of teachers who have good preventive discipline:
Well-liked Teachers (who may or may not produce high student achievement)
Provide personal attention to students
Present class activities that are fun
Maintain a relaxed atmosphere and a sense of humor
Efficient teachers (who may produce high achievement, with little student enjoyment)
Plan every detail, leaving nothing to chance
Instruct in an efficient, businesslike manner, allowing no nonsense
Maintain a strong system of rules and consequences
Expert teachers (who produce high achievement with student excitement and pleasure)
Provide an enjoyable, quality curriculum that builds student competency
Are well-organized and know what they are doing, yet remain flexible
Show that they care about students and want them to learn and behave properly
Remain quality academic and social models that students want to emulate

SUGGESTED INSTRUCTIONAL ACTIVITIES

Assignments

1. Read assigned chapter.
2. Make entries into personal notebook. Quiz, over assigned reading.

Discussion Topics

1. Take a moment to recall teachers you have had in the past. List four names: (1) the teacher you liked best, (2) your most effective teacher, (3) the teacher you most disliked, and (4) the teacher you remember as the all-around worst. (Note: write the underlined words on the chalkboard so students can remember.) Beside each name, write a few of the traits that most stand out in your mind about that teacher.

Discussion: What are the traits you best remember? They say we often teach as we have been taught: How likely are you to show in your own teaching some of the undesirable traits you have listed?

2. Take another moment to envision yourself as a teacher. List the traits you want your students to see in you. Also list traits you do not want them to see in you.
Discussion: What desired and undesired traits have you listed? Which of those traits exist naturally in your personality? Which will require some effort to enhance or eliminate?

CLASSROOMS THAT ENCOURAGE
GOOD BEHAVIOR

Classroom Components that Encourage Good Behavior

The Person Component

The Management Component -- 1. Classroom Climate

The Management Component -- 2. Classroom Routines

The Teacher Component

3. It takes time to communicate well with parents, and teachers already have heavy demands on their time. To what extent do you think communicating with parents is worth the effort and time required? (Note: Mention that teachers perceived as "best" by the community are those who take pains to communicate well with parents.)

Small-Group Collaborative Work

1. Together, compose a response to Application exercise 3 at the end of the chapter. Share your work with the class.

2. Prepare an anticipated script for Application exercise 5, including what you (the teacher) will say to James's father, what you expect him to say to you, and what you will say or suggest in return. Role-play for the class.

3. Taking into account the chapter suggestions concerning the person, management, and teacher components, outline what should be done for the situations depicted in the Scenarios in Appendix I. (Select or assign one of the following Scenarios: 1, 2, 3, 7, or 10).

TEST ITEMS

The following test items may be duplicated for classroom use.

Answers

True-False: 1.F, 2.T, 3.F, 4.T, 5.F, 6.T, 7.F, 8.F, 9.F, 10.F, 11.T, 12.F, 13.F, 14.T, 15.F, 16.F, 17.F, 18.T, 19.F, 20.F

Multiple Choice: 1.b, 2.a, 3.c, 4.c, 5.b, 6.d, 7.b, 8.b, 9.a, 10.c, 11.b, 12.a, 13.b, 14.c, 15.a, 16.c, 17.d, 18.d, 19.d, 20.c

Essay:

1. Behavior toward others seems to be related strongly to the level of respect that individuals have for themselves, respect that is likely in turn to be shown for others. The person component focuses on building such respect through three avenues: personal attention, success in learning, and recognition for accomplishment.

The management component focuses on preventing misbehavior through (1) establishment of a good working climate and (2) increased efficiency that reduces dead and awkward time which encourages misbehavior. Classroom climate is enhanced through judicious use of human relations skills; efficiency is improved through careful attention to class routines and the provision of help to students.

The teacher component has the power to reduce misbehavior through instructional efficiency, flexibility, genuine concern for students, and the provision of stimulating learning activities, all of which are seen in people referred to as "master teachers." Given such teaching, students misbehave less because they are interested and occupied and because they like and respect their teacher.

2. In (1) look for procedures by which students begin work immediately (specific activities should be named) and for quick closure and cleanup at end of lesson.

In (2) look for specific details on student movement, regrouping, or refocusing of attention.

In (3) look for specific details on the distribution and collection of materials (student assistants should be used unless there is good reason not to).

In (4) procedures should be described (as from Fredric Jones) for the use of reference models, rapid teacher circulation, and providing useful help in no more than a few seconds' time.

3. In (1) look for: clarifying Teddy's strengths and weaknesses and value as a person; placing samples of his completed and uncompleted work in the folder; documenting the frequency of specific misbehaviors you would like for Teddy to change.

In (2) look for: friendly greeting to Mr. Swett; thanking him for taking time to meet with you; reassurance that you appreciate his help as you both try to help Teddy be successful in school; seating Mr. Swett beside teacher at a table so folder can be examined easily.

In (3) look for: mention of enjoyment of Teddy's nicer qualities (enlivens class, ready wit, etc.) and review of Teddy's accomplishments in the work of the class. That should be followed by description of plans you have for Teddy's further growth (the plans make evident Teddy's shortcomings, but are couched not as criticisms but as goals).

In (4) anticipate that Mr. Swett might take a helpful attitude (e.g., "Let me know what I can do to help), or a resistant or even hostile attitude (e.g., "Some of the other boys are making him act that way; it's not his fault. I need him to work, so he doesn't have time to do all his homework. That stuff's not really important anyway"); or a noncommittal attitude ("Well, I don't know what I can do; that's up to you; do what you want").

In (5) say something like "I know both of us want what is best for Teddy. We both want him to learn and be the best person he can be. I think the plans I have made for him are good, but I need your help in order to make them work out. With both of us working together, I am certain we can help Teddy be even more successful in school."

Name_____ Date_____

True-False. All items relate to the contents of Chapter 11, "Classrooms that Encourage Good Behavior." Write T or F to the left of each item.

1. The person component has to do with the traits of the teacher as a person.

2. Recognition for accomplishment is believed to help strengthen student self-concept.

3. To strengthen self-concept, students should be congratulated for successes they might not necessarily have achieved.
4. "Esprit de corps" refers more to class morale than to traits in individual teachers.

5. Good group spirit is attainable in virtually every class, through techniques recently devised.

6. Sense of purpose in learning is enhanced through anticipation of public exhibition of results.
7. Both group gains and individual gains should be charted and displayed in the classroom.

8. Communication with parents should regularly detail both the failures and the successes of the child.
9. Peer attention to individual student achievement is to be discouraged; it promotes self-centeredness.
10. The management component refers mainly to attempts made to enhance student self-esteem.
11. Classroom climate refers to the "feeling tone" that exists in the classroom.

12. Even a good classroom climate may often be seen by the majority of students as harsh and cold.
13. Light sarcasm, used humorously, should be introduced as a means of improving classroom climate.
14. Ability to compliment genuinely was listed as one of the general human relations skills.

15. Friendliness, when not sincere, is ineffective in human relations, as its deceitfulness comes through strongly.
16. Students tend to avoid teachers who are always willing to help, because they seem to be nagging.
17. Most parents are eager to know in detail what their children are doing wrong at school.

18. Teachers should sit side-by-side with parents at a table during parent-teacher conferences.

19. If guided by teachers, parents are usually quite objective about their child's behavior.

20. Parents often ask teachers for personal advice; teachers, to build rapport, should furnish it.

All items relate to Chapter 11, "Classrooms that Encourage Good Behavior." Write the letter of the single best answer to the left of each item.

1. The person component relates mostly to (a) peers, (b) self, (c) communication, (d) cooperation.
2. Students require success that is (a) genuine, (b) hard-earned, (c) self-motivated, (d) extrinsic.
3. Esprit de corps means (a) spirited teaching, (b) happy parents, (c) group spirit, (d) contentment.
4. Class sense of purpose depends most on clear (a) rules, (b) criticism, (c) goals, (d) roles.

5. A strong motive for purposeful behavior: (a) habit, (b) public exposition, (c) criticism, (d) goal.
6. Do not display achievement gains for (a) classes, (b) schools, (c) communities, (d) individuals.
7. Parents should be regularly informed about their child's (a) misbehaviors, (b) successes, (c) shortcomings, (d) lapses of courtesy.
8. Classroom climate is most affected by (a) genetic needs, (b) management, (c) curriculum, (d) parents.
9. Classroom climate refers to (a) feeling tone, (b) aspiration, (c) organization, (d) level of respect.
10. Most valuable human relations skill: (a) sincerity, (b) listening, (c) friendliness, (d) self-respect.
11. A human relations skill that makes many people uneasy: (a) friendliness, (b) complimenting, (c) listening, (d) reinforcing.
12. To the extent practical, communications with parents should avoid statements of (a) helpful criticism, (b) expectations, (c) special programs, (d) goals.
13. The ultimate purpose of conferencing with parents is to improve (a) communication, (b) child success, (c) relationships, (d) level of support.
14. Conferences with parents should open with comments about the child's (a) areas of weakness, (b) needs, (c) good qualities, (d) record of achievement.
15. Teachers rated as most effective are usually (a) good managers, (b) highly demanding, (c) fiercely loyal to standards, (d) reluctant to compromise.
16. Good routines help by reducing (a) spontaneity, (b) variety, (c) wasted time, (d) student demands.
17. The use of student class assistants is (a) illegal, (b) discouraged, (c) required, (d) advisable.
18. Described as a "type" of teacher who may or may not produce high student achievement: (a) master, (b) efficient, (c) organized, (d) well-liked.
19. Students prize lessons that are (a) open-ended, (b) spontaneous, (c) nondirective, (d) stimulating.
20. In general, students' favorite class activities: (a) lectures, (b) directed reading, (c) cooperative group work, (d) self-guided learning.

ESSAY EXAM. Write out your responses to the following items, as directed.

1. Three components contribute strongly to proper student behavior in the classroom. They are the person component, the management component, and the teaching component. Briefly indicate how each of these components can serve a preventive function in reducing the occurrence of misbehavior.

2. Identify a subject or grade level you hope to teach. Explain how you would (1) begin and end lessons, (2) make the transition from one activity to another, (3) distribute and collect instructional materials, and (4) provide help to students during independent or group work time.

3. Suppose that you are scheduled for a routine conference with Mr. Swett, whose son Teddy (though an entertainingly cute fellow) has completed fewer than half his homework assignments and continually makes smart-aleck remarks to other students and occasionally to you, the teacher. Describe (1) how you would prepare for the conference, (2) how you would greet Mr. Swett, (3) what your opening line of discussion would be and what you would follow with, (4) three different response styles or attitudes that Mr. Swett might likely exhibit in responding to what you say, and (5) what you would say to Mr. Swett to obtain his cooperation in improving Teddy's behavior.

Chapter 12

BUILDING A PERSONAL SYSTEM OF DISCIPLINE

CHAPTER ABSTRACT

Prepackaged systems of discipline, while effective, rarely match up as well as one would like with the totality of school guidelines, student traits, and teacher philosophies, personalities, and preferred styles of teaching. Therefore, in order to promote the most effective learning environment, teachers are advised to compose personal systems of discipline tailored to their needs.

It has been the purpose of this book to help users do precisely that. Information from highly respected sources has been provided, along with practice exercises to facilitate understanding and application. Given that information, it is now relatively easy to build a personal system that will prevent misbehavior, correct misbehavior in positive ways, and promote trusting relationships between teacher and students.

Teachers begin this work already knowing a good deal about students. They know that primary-age children are very active, tire easily, become fussy, need frequent rest, and break rules regularly, even though they want to please the teacher. A major task of primary teachers is to help children become socialized to group life and school requirements and regulations.

By the time students have entered the intermediate grades, they can help establish rules and consequences of behavior. They want those rules and consequences applied consistently and impartially (except where they themselves are concerned). Students at this age are likely to argue vehemently with each other but still want to please the teacher, though they sometimes talk back when being corrected.

Middle school students are going through a difficult period in their lives, and their behavior usually reflects their inner turmoil. They are becoming increasingly rebellious and desirous of testing boundaries. Their awe of the teacher is waning, but can be replaced with respect and affection.

High school students are beginning to settle down. Some want to make the most of school; others want no part of it. Their maturity calls for teachers to relate with them on an adult basis.

In all cases, teachers must realistically accept that students are going to misbehave in school, that they will goof off, squabble, resist learning, tattle, act "cool," form disruptive cliques, and balk at doing their work. But at times those same students will be utterly caring, considerate, loving, and cooperative, providing those moments that make teaching so worthwhile.

Proceeding from a knowledge of students, personal systems of discipline should be built on the understanding that discipline is comprised of three important facets, called preventive, supportive, and corrective. Each facet plays an indispensable role in good classroom behavior.

Preventive discipline, used to forestall misbehavior, is based on good classroom climate, interesting curriculum, stimulating teaching, good rules of behavior, teaching students how they are expected to behave, and an affective means of invoking consequences when rules are broken.

Supportive discipline, which helps keep students on task, makes good use of signals, proximity, interest in student work, restructuring of difficult work, flexibility, humor, and encouragement.

When misbehavior occurs despite good prevention and support, corrective discipline is needed to stop and redirect improper behavior positively while maintaining the best possible relations between teacher and students.

Specific guidance for composing a personal system of discipline is provided in the text and is summarized in the instructors' discussion notes which follow.

INSTRUCTORS' DISCUSSION NOTES

Use Transparency 16 to guide discussion.

STUDENTS require discipline for desirable learning and social development.
TEACHERS require discipline in order to teach well.

DISCIPLINE is best accomplished through a comprehensive plan that gives
        attention to Preventive, Supportive, and Corrective measures

   Regarding PREVENTIVE DISCIPLINE, used to forestall misbehavior
        Try to help students meet their needs for belonging, power, freedom, and fun
        Make your curriculum as enjoyable and worthwhile for students as possible
        Collaborate with students to formulate rules and consequences of classroom
            behavior
        Continually emphasize and exemplify in your own behavior good manners and the
            golden rule, by doing things such as . . .

   Regarding SUPPORTIVE DISCIPLINE, used when minor misbehavior occurs
        Get students back on track through signals, expressions, and gestures, such as . . .
        Show interest in student work, by observing, commenting, and discussing
        Restructure work that is too difficult
        Relieve tension by injecting humor, such as . . .
        Temporarily remove seductive objects from students

   Regarding CORRECTIVE DISCIPLINE, used when behavior rules are violated
        Invoke a consequence commensurate with the misbehavior
        Follow through consistently
        Redirect misbehavior positively, in ways such as . . .
        Invoke insubordination or severe clause when appropriate, such as in . . .

Steps in Preparing a Good Discipline Plan
1. Specify teacher and student needs and tentatively set limits--for example . . .
2. Discuss with students behavior that will best serve the class, such as . . .
3. With student collaboration, write out rules and consequences, such as . . .
4. Establish a support system of administrator, parents, and fellow teacher . . .
5. Plan what you will do for preventive and supportive discipline--for example . .
6. Teach and model responsible behavior, by . . .
7. Decide how to invoke consequences positively when rules are broken, e.g., . . .
8. Continually evaluate the plan and modify it as necessary, by . . .

SUGGESTED INSTRUCTIONAL ACTIVITIES

Assignment

1. Read Chapters 12 and 13 and be prepared to discuss their contents in class.

2. Review your notebooks and highlight points you now intend to include in your personal system of discipline.

Discussion Topics

1. Did the sequence of steps suggested for building your personal system of discipline seem realistic and helpful? Explain.

2. To what extent did you find helpful the descriptions of typical behavior patterns of primary, intermediate, middle school, and high school students?

3. Which of the discipline systems in Chapter 13 did you find most attractive? What would you change about it/them to better meet your personal needs?

4. Do you now have a fairly good idea of how to proceed in putting together a system of discipline that matches your preferences and the realities of the situation in which you might be likely to teach? Discuss any concerns or questions you might have.

(Note 1: Students always want to know first what you expect the personal system to include and how long you want the written paper to be. The personal system can be described adequately in approximately five typewritten pages, double-spaced. Tell students you want the paper to cover (1) the class [grade level, subject, social realities], (2) the preventive, supportive, and corrective aspects of the system, (3) how administrative and fellow teacher support for the system will be obtained, and (4) how the program will be communicated to students and parents.)

(Note 2: Some students will ask about schoolwide systems of discipline and whether or not their plan should reflect such systems. Tell them that for the purpose of this class they should have the experience of composing a plan of their own, based entirely on what they believe would be most effective for them.)

Small-Group Collaborative Work

1. Review the cumulative list of discipline concepts presented in Appendix II, testing each other to ensure understanding.

2. Discuss questions or concerns that might exist regarding composing the personal system of discipline. Concerns that cannot be resolved within the group should be brought to the attention of the entire class.

Ongoing Class Work

Students' main responsibility is now to complete their personal systems of discipline. Suggest that they consult the models presented in Chapter 13. Assure students that this assignment is not a competition where they are judged against each other, but is intended rather to enable each person to compose a complete and thoughtful system that will work in the situation for which it is designed.

It is helpful to schedule a series of personal conferences with students for answering questions and appraising their approach to the assignment.

FINAL EVALUATION

You may wish to conduct a formal review of the discipline concepts presented in Appendix II.

Some instructors give final exams; others do not, feeling that the final paper (personal system of discipline) is the ultimate measure of students' performance.

Evaluation should be done in keeping with the criteria presented at the beginning of the class, or as those criteria might have been modified during the progress of the course.

PREPARING PERSONAL SYSTEMS OF DISCIPLINE

STUDENTS require discipline for ...

TEACHERS require discipline in order to ...

PREVENTIVE DISCIPLINE

SUPPORTIVE DISCIPLINE

CORRECTIVE DISCIPLINE

STEPS IN PREPARING A GOOD DISCIPLINE SYSTEM

SELECTED LIST OF CONCEPTS IN DISCIPLINE
(See Appendix II in the text for a comprehensive list.)

active listening
activity reinforcers
appreciative praise
autocratic teacher
behavior modification
behavior shaping
behavior window
behaviorally at risk
body language
boss teacher
classroom meetings
consequences
correcting by directing
democratic teacher
dignity
displaying inadequacy
efficient help
evaluative praise
genuine goal of belonging
getting attention
Grandma's rule
hidden asset
I-messages
incentives
insubordination rule
lead teacher
logical consequences
misbehavior
mistaken goals
no-lose conflict resolution
nonassertive response style
overlapping
participative classroom management
permissive teacher
positive consequences
positive reinforcement
primary feelings
problem ownership

professionals and clients
punishment
quality curriculum
reality appraisal
reinforcement
reinforcing stimulus
responsibility versus obedience
roadblocks to Assertive Discipline
roadblocks to communication
rules-ignore-praise (RIP)
rules-reward-punishment (RRP)
sane messages
satiation
schedules of reinforcement
secondary feelings
setting limits
short-term solutions
situational assistance
social contract
social reinforcers
student accountability
student roles
students' five basic needs
students' rights
successive approximations
supporting self-control
tangible reinforcers
teacher roles
teachers at their best
teachers at their worst
teachers' rights
threats vs. promises
three dimensions of discipline
token economies
win-lose conflict resolution
withitness
you-messages